FOR THE LOVE OF ACT SCIENCE

by Michael Cerro

Published by Private Prep

Printed by CreateSpace, An Amazon.com Company

Cover art by Ryan Lause

ACKNOWLEDGMENTS

I would like to dedicate this page of the guide to the following people for making this journey possible.

To my mother and father, for always supporting me throughout my life. I love the both of you dearly.

To my younger sister Nina and younger brother Stephen, for looking up to me just as much as I look up to the both of you.

To my aunts and grandmothers, for being my guardian angels.

To my uncles and grandfathers, for teaching me the meaning of hard work.

To my mentor Jeremy Cohen, for giving me every opportunity to succeed.

To Scott Levenson and Steve Feldman, for teaching me how leadership comes from the heart.

To my "Test-Prep-Better-Half" Heidi Fisher, for being an amazing verbal specialist throughout the years. Working alongside you is a blessing.

To the original AJA team: Adam Dressler, Jonathan Weed, and Andrew Burten, for teaching me what it means to be a test prep professional.

To the new AJAM members: Michele O'Brien, Andrew Dahl, Ilan Caplan, Kalyan Ray-Mazumder, Kyla Haggerty, and Tehya Baxter—working with all of you is a privilege each and every day.

To the editors of this guide: Chance Gautney and Jackson Shain, your recommendations were invaluable. Thank you.

To Lindsay Bressman, for all your efforts in helping me brand this guide.

To all the Private Prep Long Island directors: Stacy Berlin, Jen Morganstern, Jenny La Monica, Allyson Stumacher, and Shana Wallace, for your immense support with every family.

To everyone in the Private Prep family, you are all amazing!

To "The Crew": Stephen Dagnell, John Castles, Paarus Sohi, James Panagos, Lou Marinos, Charlie Castillo, Jared Levy, Mike Ryan, Tim Kolchinskiy, and Stan Shvartsberg, for being the most incredible group of friends. You gentlemen mean the world to me.

To my dear friend, Bernadette Vingerhoets. The world I see is always brighter with you around.

And to my best friend (and diagram creator) David Hintz, for continuing to push me towards new heights. We're just getting started.

Contents

How a Children's Book Taught Me ACT Science

I started tutoring math and science part-time during the summer of 2011 as a side job while completing my Master's degree. At that time I was on my way to medical school when I suddenly found myself falling in love with tutoring, especially SAT and ACT preparation. After some heavy consideration, I decided to embark on this journey full-time, fine-tuning my skills as a tutor. Then, while tutoring privately I discovered Private Prep, a tutoring company based in New York, and began tutoring full-time in the fall of 2012. As the spring of my first school year approached I found myself seeing more and more students, eventually reaching a peak of around 30 per week. Given all my experience, the partners of the company asked me to join their training team and write a guide of what was to become the ACT Science section. So, I did. I took what resources we currently had, gave myself one week to go through all of them, and developed the first iteration of the ACT Science Strategy Guide. It was raw and needed a lot of fine tuning but it was a start. Still, I knew I needed to gain even more experience. The following school year I pushed to tutor even more, and each year since have striven to eclipse the year before; I knew this would be my path to gaining more knowledge, and eventually sharing it.

The more I tutored, the more consistencies I found in ACT Science. Each year I added more to the guide and came up with better ways to train new tutors. But, I still felt I was missing an overall approach, the glue to tie all of the strategies together. I wanted to be able to capture the essence of ACT Science in just one sentence. Finally, in the spring of 2013, I found my answer. I had the pleasure of working with a student who was scoring approximately five to six points higher on ACT Science than any other section, which is atypical. During one of our lessons I asked the student why he thought this was the case. His response was, "It's like the book Where's Waldo. There is absolute chaos happening on the page, but your main job is just to find Waldo." Brilliant, I thought! I finally had my answer (If you are unfamiliar with this children's book, please search the internet for pictures. It will make my message clearer!).

When you work through the problems of this guide I encourage you to remember these words of wisdom. This is the only section, SAT or ACT, where the answer is staring right at you. You simply need to find it. Do not try to use comprehension, do not try to understand what the experiments are about, just...find Waldo. This is a section that tests your ability to understand what is important, to know what is not important, to use logic and deductive reasoning, to move efficiently, and to dismiss fatigue (it is the last section after all!). Once that mindset sinks in, I guarantee you will be happy with your score increases.

Please reach out to me at michael@privateprep.com if you have any questions. I would wish you the best of luck on your journey to improve, but you won't need it. You are already a bright student with a craving to improve–you just need the right approach. I am humbled by this opportunity to show you what I believe to be the most efficient route to what you are seeking.

For science!

CHAPTER 1

THE BASICS

1.1 The Types of Passages

> " *Be formless. Shapeless. Like water.* " — BRUCE LEE

Most ACT Science study guides will inform you that there are three different passage types in the following formats:

PASSAGE TYPE	AMOUNT IN SECTION	NUMBER OF QUESTIONS
Data Representation	3	5
Research Summary	3	6
Conflicting Viewpoints	1	7

This analysis is not wrong, but it's also not completely correct. The ACT is forever changing, and you need to be adaptable on the day of your exam. The structure shown above has been dependable for many years. However, in late 2014 and early 2015, the structure shifted. Instead, those exams contained 6 passages in total, not 7, and each passage had one more question than you would anticipate. This is the ACT afterall, so curveballs should be expected every now and then. Fortunately for us, these changes really do not effect us. The approach in this book ensures that you will be prepared for structural changes.

We will be tackling the ACT Science section with the following structure in mind:

PASSAGE TYPE	AMOUNT IN SECTION	NUMBER OF QUESTIONS
Conflicting Viewpoints	1, maybe 2?	7, maybe 8?
Everything Else	The Rest	5-7

This may seem silly, but having a flexible structure will allow you to mentally adjust to whatever structure is presented on test day. The conflicting viewpoints passage has a certain approach (you will know this passage when you see it), but the others all follow the same methods. Do not worry too much about the structure of the section. Worry about the tactics.

If it will put your mind at ease to know how many passages are in a particular section, this information is often stated in the first sentence of the directions at the beginning of the section.

> **DIRECTIONS:** There are seven passages in this test. Each passage is followed by several questions. After reading a passage, choose the best answer to each question and fill in the corresponding oval on your answer document. You may refer to the passages as often as necessary.
> You are NOT permitted to use a calculator on this test.

1.2   Locators, Locators, Locators

> " *Always go back to the passage with a purpose.* "

If you read nothing else but this one section you will probably improve your science score. The most important part of properly tackling ACT Science is **knowing where to look first**. We cannot stress this enough. In order to figure out where to look first, attempt to locate the following "first locators" in the question:

- Figure 1, Figure 2, Table 1, Table 2, etc. - Your most important locator. This is your starting point for most questions.

- "Based on the results of study..." - Look at the data of a particular study.

- "Based on study...." - Your locator could be in the text of the study, or the data.

- "According to the information provided", "According to the passage", "Based on the passage" - Your locator is in the text.

Once you have identified where to look, the next step is **knowing what to look for**. This is your *Waldo*, or "second locators". Do not go back to the passage without a purpose. Attempt to locate the following in the question and passage:

- Units - m, s, kg, N, etc. Your most important second locator.

- Science terminology - pH, temperature bath, detector, deposit - Any phrase that pops out and feels different from the directions of the question.

- X and Y axes labels

- Answer choices. Sometimes your best locator is found by comparing the key phrases of the choices.

Develop the habit of finding your first and second locators before attempting to solve each question. Doing so will improve your speed and efficiency when going through the ACT science section. In addition, your accuracy on early questions will be nearly flawless and you will use less energy when answering questions. All of the preceding locators matter when handling the last section of your ACT.

Your Objective: Circle the first and second locators in the questions and answer choices below. Then, circle the corresponding locators in the passage.

LOCATOR EXAMPLE 1

Experiment 1

A student decided to perform a titration experiment to neutralize a HCl solution. 50 mL of a 3 mmole/mL HCl solution was poured into a beaker and placed under a *buret* (a tall, thin, graduated cylinder with a stop valve at the bottom). The buret was filled with the NaOH solution. The student slightly opened the stop valve on the buret and recorded the pH using various indicators. She recorded her results in the table below.

Table 1	
Volume of NaOH (mL)	pH of solution
0	3
2	5
4	6
6	7

Experiment 2

Next, the student poured an unknown solution, *USX*, into the beaker and measured the pH. She recorded her results in Table 2.

Table 2	
Volume of USX (mL)	pH of solution
0	7
2	4
4	2
6	2

QUESTIONS

1. Based on Table 1, as the volume of NaOH increased, the pH of the solution:
   A. increased only.
   B. decreased only.
   C. remained constant.
   D. cannot be determined from the given information.

2. The student hypothesized that as the amount of USX increased in the beaker, the pH of the solution would increase. Do the results of Experiment 2 support this hypothesis?
   F. Yes, as the volume of USX increased the pH of the solution increased.
   G. Yes, as the volume of USX increased the pH of the solution decreased.
   H. No, as the volume of USX increased the pH of the solution increased.
   J. No, as the volume of USX increased the pH of the solution decreased.

3. Based on the passage, if 100 mL of HCl was used instead of 50 mL, how many mmole of HCl would be present in the beaker before the start of the titration?
   A. 3 mmole
   B. 50 mmole
   C. 100 mmole
   D. 300 mmole

1.3 Number Behavior: Trends in Tables and Figures

" *It is not about the actual numbers, it is about how they behave.* "

When looking at a table or figure, develop a habit of instantly identifying trends. This will allow you to interpet data with speed and ensure that you are ready for many of the basic questions presented on the ACT Science section. More importantly, do not concern yourself with the numbers themselves. More advanced questions are looking to test whether or not you can develop trends between different variables and then correlate these trends with the correct answer choice.

Your Objective: Identify the appropriate trends and answer the questions in the following examples.

TRENDS EXAMPLE 1

Table 1				
Trial	mass (kg)	a (m/s^2)	T (°C)	F (N)
1	2	3	25	6
2	6	3	25	18
3	10	3	25	30
4	14	3	25	42
5	2	3	25	6
6	2	6	25	12
7	2	12	25	24
8	2	24	25	48
9	2	3	25	6
10	2	3	27	3.7
11	2	3	29	2.4
12	2	3	31	1.9

Table 2		
Weeks	Pesticide Concentration (kg/m^3)	Biomass (kg)
1	22	151
2	49	177
3	51	180
4	28	162

QUESTIONS

4. Based on Table 1, as mass increases, F:
   F. increases only.
   G. decreases only.
   H. remains constant.
   J. varies, but with no general.

5. Based on Table 1, as a increases, F:
   A. increases only.
   B. decreases only.
   C. remains constant.
   D. varies, but with no general.

6. Based on Table 1, as T increases, F:
   F. increases only.
   G. decreases only.
   H. remains constant.
   J. varies, but with no general.

7. Based on Table 2, as the number of weeks increase, the pesticide concentration:
   A. increases only.
   B. decreases only.
   C. remains constant.
   D. varies, but with no general.

8. Based on Table 2, as pesticide concentration increases, biomass:
   F. increases only.
   G. decreases only.
   H. remains constant.
   J. varies, but with no general.

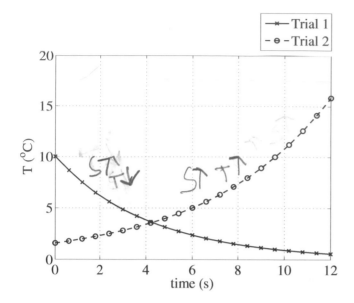

Figure 1

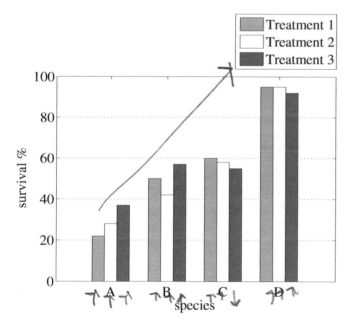

Figure 2

9. According to Figure 1, for Trial 1, as time increases, temperature:
    A. increases only.
    B. decreases only.
    C. remains constant.
    D. varies, but with no general.

10. According to Figure 1, for Trial 2, as time increases, temperature:
    F. increases only.
    G. decreases only.
    H. remains constant.
    J. varies, but with no general.

11. According to Figure 2, as species A underwent each successive treatment, the percent that survived:
    A. increased only.
    B. decreased only.
    C. remained constant.
    D. varied, but with no general.

12. According to Figure 2, as species B underwent each successive treatment, the percent that survived:
    F. increased only.
    G. decreased only.
    H. remained constant.
    J. varied, but with no general.

13. According to Figure 2, as species C underwent each successive treatment, the percent that survived:
    A. increased only.
    B. decreased only.
    C. remained constant.
    D. varied, but with no general.

14. According to Figure 2, as species D underwent each successive treatment, the percent that survived:
    F. increased only.
    G. decreased only.
    H. remained constant.
    J. varied, but with no general.

1.4 Math

$$\textit{Don't be a mathematician, be a scientist.}$$
""

There was a joke we commonly told while I was obtaining my engineering degree: "Mathematicians calculate π as 3.14159..., engineers calculate π as 3.14, and scientists calculate π as approximately 3." In the ACT science section, when you come across a problem that requires simple math, do not be exact with your calculation. The answer choices are forgiving and the test-makers want you to round, to estimate, and approximate. Let's look at a mini-example together:

MATH EXAMPLE 1

Table 1	
Time for water runoff (sec)	629

QUESTIONS

15. According to Table 1, approximately how many *minutes* did it take for the water to runoff?
    A. 5
    B. 10
    C. 20
    D. 40

The goal of this example is to convert 629 seconds into minutes. First, we should know that 60 seconds is equivalent to 1 minute. Next, decide how to go about doing the calculation. 629 is not a pretty number to work with, so let's round! Give yourself -200 points if you rounded it to 630 in your mind. Round more! Let's try rounding to 600 and then performing the calculation.

$$\frac{629}{60} \quad \to \quad \frac{600}{60} \quad \to \quad \frac{60}{6} \quad \to \quad 10$$

Notice that when you use rounded multiples of 10, the zeros cancel out and make your calculations much easier. The lesson here: round, then round some more!

Your Objective: Here are a set of math drills to help you practice estimation. Do NOT use your calculator and do not try to obtain exact answers. The goal here is to do these calculations swiftly with just your pencil.

m1. How many minutes are in 1249 seconds?
m2. What is 9 times 14?
m3. What is 120 times 2.5?
m4. What is 10% of 52?
m5. How many days are in 22 weeks?
m6. How many inches are there in 99 feet?
m7. What is 50% of 3,933?

m8. What is 11 times 55?
m9. What is 162 divided by 50?
m10. How many hours are there in July?
m11. What is 10% of 244?
m12. What is 100,111 divided by 101?
m13. How many seconds are there in 12 minutes?
m14. What is 19 times 302?

Michael Cerro | 15

1.5 Extrapolation and Estimation

There will be questions on the ACT Science section that require you to extend the trend of a figure or table beyond its given boundaries. For line graphs, **extend the line with your pencil** to ensure the best estimation. The ACT is very good at anticipating incorrect answer choices that look correct when you only glance to extrapolate the line. For tables or bar graphs, look for the best answer choice that fits your drawn estimation. The majority of these questions **have only one answer choice that fits the correct range**. For example, if you deduce that the correct answer should be between 1 cm and 4 cm and there are two answer choices available in that range, you have likely done something wrong.

Your Objective: Answer the extrapolation questions in the examples below.

EXTRAPOLATION EXAMPLE 1

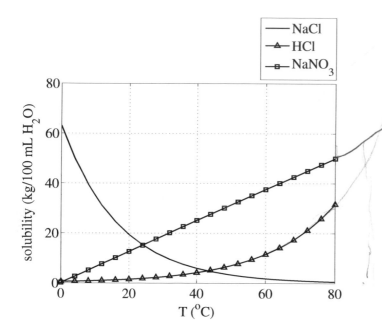

Figure 1

Table 1			
Trial	block mass (kg)	incline $\theta(°)$	block speed (m/s)
1	4	30	1.7
2	6	30	2.2
3	8	30	2.4
4	6	40	3.7
5	6	45	4.4
6	6	50	4.8

QUESTIONS

16. According to Figure 1, at 90°C, the mass of $NaNO_3$ that is soluble in 100 mL of H_2O is:
- F. less than 35 kg.
- G. between 35 kg and 40 kg.
- H. between 45 kg and 55 kg.
- J. greater than 55 kg.

17. According to Figure 1, at -10°C, the mass of NaCl that is soluble in 100 mL of H_2O is:
- A. less than 0 kg.
- B. between 0 kg and 30 kg.
- C. between 30 kg and 60 kg.
- D. greater than 60 kg.

18. According to Figure 1, at 100°C, the mass of HCl that is soluble in 100 mL of H_2O is:
- F. less than 0 kg.
- G. between 0 kg and 30 kg.
- H. between 30 kg and 60 kg.
- J. greater than 60 kg.

19. Suppose Trial 3 had been repeated with a block mass of 10 kg. According to Table 1, the block speed measured would most likely have been:
- A. less than 1.7 m/s.
- B. between 1.7 m/s and 2.2 m/s.
- C. between 2.2 m/s and 2.4 m/s.
- D. greater than 2.4 m/s.

20. Suppose Trial 4 had been repeated with an incline elevation of 35°. According to Table 1, the block speed measured would most likely have been:
- F. less than 3.7 m/s.
- G. between 3.7 m/s and 4.4 m/s.
- H. between 4.4 m/s and 4.8 m/s.
- J. greater than 4.8 m/s.

1.6 The Data Bridge

> " *Find what the data have in common ... that's your bridge.* "

The **Data Bridge** skill links multiple figures or tables to arrive at the correct answer and has a similar feel to the transitive property in mathematics. Here is how you can identify that you will be using this skill and what to do after you've recognized the question type:

DATA BRIDGE EXAMPLE 1

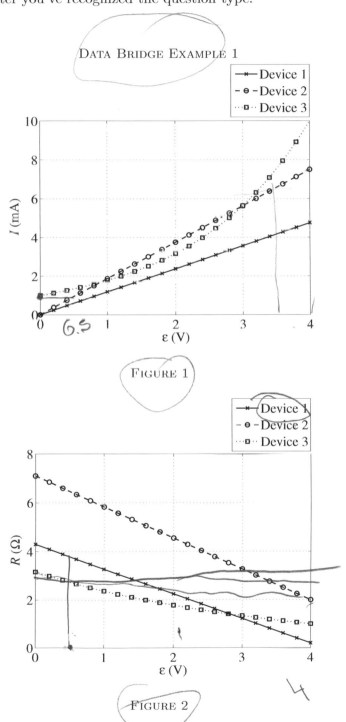

FIGURE 1

FIGURE 2

EXPLANATION

21. Based on Figures 1 and 2, when the resistance of Device 2 is 3 Ω, the current, I, is approximately:
A. 3 mA.
B. 4 mA.
C. 5 mA.
D. 6 mA.

Notice how the question mentions multiple figures, "Figures 1 and 2". Whenever a question mentions multiple figures and/or tables it is probably calling for you to apply the Data Bridge tactic.

The key locator of the question is 3 Ω. This unit (Ω) is located in Figure 2. For Device 2, Figure 2 yields a value of approximately 3.25 V. The voltage (V) is our *bridge* because it is located in both figures. The bridge variable, typically, will appear on the same axis throughout all data. In this example voltage is on the x-axis of both figures.

Next, we use 3.25 V in Figure 1 for Device 2 and find the current (I) to be approximately 6 mA. The correct answer is choice D.

Try it again:

22. Based on Figures 1 and 2, when the current of Device 1 is 1 mA, the resistance is approximately:
F. 2 Ω.
G. 3 Ω.
H. 4 Ω.
J. 5 Ω.

Your Objective: Answer the following questions by using the Data Bridge skill.

Data Bridge Example 2

Table 1	
Rock cluster	Av percentage
I	20%
II	40%
III	60%
IV	80%

Table 2	
Av percentage	Power (W)
10%	593
30%	482
50%	361
70%	244

Questions

23. Based on Tables 1 and 2, a power of 300 W is most likely associated with which rock cluster?
   A. Rock cluster I
   B. Rock cluster II
   C. Rock cluster III
   D. Rock cluster IV

24. Based on Tables 1 and 2, which rock cluster most likely has the greatest power?
   F. Rock cluster I
   G. Rock cluster II
   H. Rock cluster III
   J. Rock cluster IV

25. Based on Tables 1 and 2, which of the following values is closest to the power of Rock cluster II?
   A. 250 W
   B. 350 W
   C. 435 W
   D. 500 W

26. Which variable represents the *bridge*?
   F. Rock cluster
   G. Av percentage
   H. Power
   J. None of the above

1.7   Chapter Test: The Basics

The chapter test you are about to complete will test your knowledge of the skills introduced throughout Chapter One. We recommend timing yourself and seeing how quickly you can traverse through the questions. Your eventual goal should be the 35 minutes allotted for the actual science section of the ACT, but do not rush to hit that mark just yet. (If you have timing accommodations, shoot for that goal instead!) Simply have a clock running to see how long it takes you to complete 40 questions. If you are using the proper mindset, finding your *Waldos*, and refraining from over-thinking the questions, you should come close to that mark.

Here are some simple tips to help you move faster on this science section, or any other science section you take:

1. Do not worry about reading the passages first. Instead, go straight to the questions. You will find your first locators in the questions. Know what you are looking for before you look for it.

2. Questions within a single passage get harder as you progress. Do not spend much time trying to figure out the last questions. If you must, guess and move on.

3. If you catch yourself getting lost or trying to understand the nuances of the experiment, stop, reset, and tackle the question from the start.

4. Remember your training. You've learned a great deal from the first chapter of this guide – apply it.

5. *The ACT is always changing and keeping us guessing. So, in the spirit of the ACT, there will be some questions that grab skills from later chapters in this book. This is an opportunity to prove to yourself that ACT Science is not that bad! You're welcome.

Good luck!

SCIENCE
35 Minutes—40 Questions

DIRECTIONS: There are six passages in this test. Each passage is followed by several questions. After reading a passage, choose the best answer to each question and fill in the corresponding oval on your answer document. You may refer to the passages as often as necessary.

You are NOT permitted to use a calculator on this test.

Passage I

Researchers studied the effectiveness of different stimuli and the ability to smell of normal cockroaches compared to cockroaches lacking a protein required to detect a wide range of odors.

Study 1

Three mazes were constructed, each containing a dish with a 10% sugar medium at the far end. In each maze, one of three stimuli was sprayed near the sugar medium, either: lemon oil, 5% acetic acid, or 35% ethanol. No additional substances were added to the mazes. Then, 10 normal cockroaches were placed in each maze. The average time for the cockroaches to reach the end of each maze was determined. The results are tabulated below (see Table 1).

Table 1: Normal cockroaches	
Stimulus introduced	Time to reach medium (s)
Lemon oil	15
5% acetic acid	27
35% ethanol	18

Study 2

The same three mazes were again constructed, each containing a dish with a 10% sugar medium at the far end. In each maze one of three stimuli was sprayed near the sugar medium, either: lemon oil, 5% acetic acid, or 35% ethanol. No additional substances were added to the mazes. Then, 10 cockroaches lacking a necessary protein to detect a wide range of odors were placed in each maze. The average time for the cockroaches to reach the end of each maze was determined. The results are tabulated below (see Table 2).

Table 2: Abnormal cockroaches	
Stimulus introduced	Time to reach medium (s)
Lemon oil	30
5% acetic acid	55
35% ethanol	41

Study 3

Study 1 was repeated using different concentrations of acetic acid: 2%, 5%, and 10%. The results are tabulated below (see Table 3).

Table 3	
Stimulus introduced	Time to reach medium (s)
2% acetic acid	15
5% acetic acid	27
10% acetic acid	48

1. According to the results of Study 1, which stimuli proved to be most effective in attracting the cockroaches?
   A. Lemon Oil
   B. 5% acetic acid
   C. 35% ethanol
   D. Cannot be determined from the given information.

2. Based on Table 3, as the concentration of acetic acid increased, the time to reach the medium:
   F. increased only.
   G. decreased only.
   H. remained constant.
   J. varied, but with no general trend.

3. A researcher wanted to reproduce a study that yielded the *slowest* time to reach the medium. According to the results of Studies 1 and 2, the researcher would construct a study containing:
   A. normal cockroaches and a lemon oil stimulus.
   B. abnormal cockroaches and a lemon oil stimulus.
   C. normal cockroaches and a 5% acetic acid stimulus.
   D. abnormal cockroaches and a 5% acetic acid stimulus.

4. Suppose an additional trial in Study 3 had been performed using a 7% acetic acid stimulus. According to Table 3, the time for the normal cockroaches to reach the medium would most likely have been:
   F. less than 15 seconds.
   G. between 15 and 27 seconds.
   H. between 27 and 48 seconds.
   J. greater than 48 seconds.

5. Based on Table 2, how many *minutes*, on average, did it take the cockroaches to reach the medium when exposed to lemon oil?
   A. 0.25 minutes
   B. 0.50 minutes
   C. 0.75 minutes
   D. 1.00 minutes

6. Suppose an additional trial in Study 1 had been performed using a 40% ethanol stimulus. Assume changing the concentration of ethanol yields the same effect as changing the concentration of acetic acid. Based on Studies 1 and 3, the time for the normal cockroaches to reach the medium would most likely have been:
   F. less than 15 seconds.
   G. between 15 and 16.5 seconds.
   H. between 16.5 and 18 seconds.
   J. greater than 18 seconds.

7. Suppose Study 3 had been repeated using abnormal cockroaches instead of normal cockroaches. Based on the results of Studies 1 and 2, how would this change the results of Study 3? The time for the cockroaches to reach the sugar medium would:
   A. decrease for all stimuli tested.
   B. increase for all stimuli tested.
   C. both decrease and increase depending on the stimuli tested.
   D. not change for any stimuli tested.

Passage II

Students recorded data on the various thermal properties of liquid water, H_2O, at 1 atmosphere (atm) of pressure.

Figures 1-3 each show a property of water at different temperatures. The *density* of water, which is defined as the mass per unit volume, is displayed in Figure 1 at various temperatures. The *absolute pressure* of water, which is the pressure measured relative to the absolute zero pressure, is displayed in Figure 2 at various temperatures. The specific entropy, which measures the availability of energy of the molecules, is displayed in Figure 3 at various temperatures.

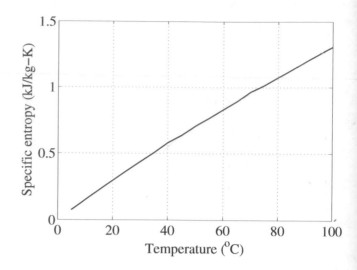

Figure 3

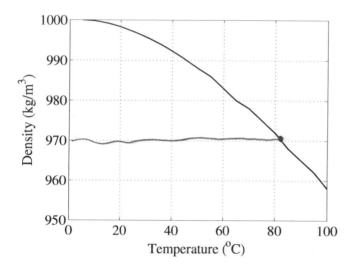

Figure 1

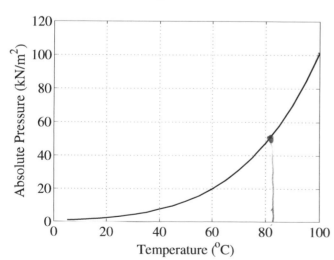

Figure 2

8. According to Figure 1, at 1 atm, as temperature increases, the density of water:
   F. increases only.
   G. decreases only.
   H. increases, then decreases.
   J. decreases, then increases.

9. According to Figure 2, at 1 atm, as temperature increases, the absolute pressure of water:
   A. increases only.
   B. decreases only.
   C. increases, then decreases.
   D. decreases, then increases.

10. According to Figure 3, at 1 atm, as temperature increases, the specific entropy of water:
    F. increases only.
    G. decreases only.
    H. increases, then decreases.
    J. decreases, then increases.

11. According to Figure 2, at 1 atm, a temperature of 130°C would most likely yield an absolute pressure:
    A. less than 80 kN/m².
    B. between 80 and 100 kN/m².
    C. between 100 and 120 kN/m².
    D. greater than 120 kN/m².

12. Based on Figures 1 and 2, at 1 atm, water with a density of 970 kg/m^3 will have an absolute pressure closest to which of the following?

    F. 10 kN/m^2

    G. 30 kN/m^2

    H. 50 kN/m^2

    J. 70 kN/m^2

13. According to Figure 3, at 1 atm, a temperature of 110°C would most likely yield a specific entropy of:

    A. less than 1 kJ/kg-K.

    B. between 1 and 1.25 kJ/kg-K.

    C. between 1.25 and 1.5 kJ/kg-K.

    D. greater than 1.5 kJ/kg-K.

14. A student was asked to choose the variable that best exhibited a linear relationship with respect to temperature. Based on Figures 1-3, the student should choose:

    F. density.

    G. absolute pressure.

    H. specific entropy.

    J. none of the above.

Passage III

Students tabulated data regarding the fall time of different toy objects sliding down an inclined plane.

In each trial, the students released a toy from rest and recorded the time it took to fall down the inclined plane over various surfaces. The toy objects tested were a sphere, a cube, and a pyramid, all made of wood and having roughly the same mass of 2.0 kg. The surfaces tested were sandpaper, wood, and glass. The students recorded their results in Table 1.

Trial	Object	Surface	Time (s)
1	Sphere	Sandpaper	5.4
2	Sphere	Wood	4.7
3	Sphere	Glass	3.3
4	Cube	Sandpaper	7.9
5	Cube	Wood	6.2
6	Cube	Glass	5.5
7	Pyramid	Sandpaper	8.1
8	Pyramid	Wood	6.3
9	Pyramid	Glass	5.4

15. According to the data, as the experiment progressed from Trial 1 to Trial 3, the time it took for the toy object to reach the bottom of the inclined plane:
   A. increased only.
   B. decreased only.
   C. increased, then decreased.
   D. decreased, then increased.

16. According to the data, as the experiment progressed from Trial 7 to Trial 9, the time it took for the toy object to reach the bottom of the inclined plane:
   F. increased only.
   G. decreased only.
   H. increased, then decreased.
   J. decreased, then increased.

17. According to the passage, if 5 toy spheres were placed on a balance, the balance reading would most likely be closest to which of the following?
   A. 5 kg
   B. 8 kg
   C. 10 kg
   D. 13 kg

18. Based on the results of the study, the object that experienced the fastest *speed* sliding down the inclined plane occurred during:
   F. Trial 1.
   G. Trial 3.
   H. Trial 4.
   J. Trial 7.

19. Suppose an additional trial had been conducted using a sphere and a *brick* surface. If the time for the sphere to reach the bottom of the brick inclined plane was 3.8 seconds, based on the data, approximately how long would it take for a cube to reach the bottom of the brick inclined plane?
   A. Less than 5.5 seconds
   B. Between 5.5 and 6.2 seconds
   C. Between 6.2 and 7.9 seconds.
   D. More than 7.9 seconds

20. Suppose the experiment were repeated except the objects were made of glass. Based on the data and other information given, how would the time for the glass objects to reach the bottom of the inclined plane compare to the results tabulated for the original objects?
   F. The time for the glass objects to reach the bottom would be greater for all surfaces.
   G. The time for the glass objects to reach the bottom of the inclined plane would be less for all surfaces.
   H. The time for the glass objects to reach the bottom would be greater for some surfaces, and less for others.
   J. Cannot be determined from the information given.

Passage IV

Researchers conducted a study to see if various parameters, such as proximity and pH, altered radiation levels in waters near nuclear power plants.

Study 1

Three different water sources near a nuclear power plant in North Carolina, United States were chosen to test for radiation levels. The researchers collected a 100 mL sample of water from each source and determined the pH using titration methods. The distance from the power plant and pH levels are shown in Table 1.

Table 1		
Water Source	Distance (m)	pH
1	20	6.7
2	25	7.0
3	30	7.2

Study 2

The researchers left a measuring probe in the three water sources for 20 days, which recorded radiation to the nearest *milligray* (mG) once a day. Their results are shown in Figure 1.

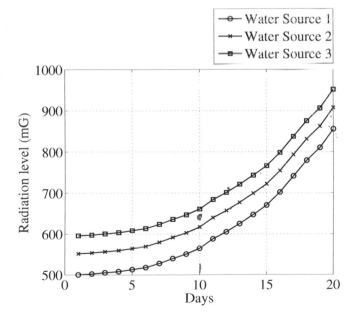

Figure 1

21. According to Table 1, as the distance from the power plant increased, the pH level:
    A. increased.
    B. decreased.
    C. increased, then decreased.
    D. cannot be determined.

22. According to Figure 1, as the number of days increased, the radiation level:
    F. increased for all water sources.
    G. decreased for all water sources.
    H. increased for some water sources, and decreased for others.
    J. iecreased for some water sources, and decreased for others.

23. According to the data, as the pH level increased, the radiation level:
    A. increased.
    B. decreased.
    C. varied, but with no general trend.
    D. stayed constant.

24. According to the data, as the distance from the power plant increased, the radiation level:
    F. increased.
    G. decreased.
    H. increased, then decreased.
    J. remained constant.

25. Suppose the study was allowed to take place an additional 5 days. Based on the results of Study 2, the radiation level for Water Source 2 after an additional 5 days would most likely have been:
    A. less than 850 mG
    B. between 850 mG and 900 mG.
    C. between 900 mG and 950 mG.
    D. greater than 950 mG.

26. Suppose an additional water source was discovered at a distance 27 m from the power plant. If Study 2 were repeated, the radiation level for this water source after 10 days would be approximately:
    F. less than 550 mG.
    G. between 550 mG and 600 mG.
    H. between 600 mG and 650 mG.
    J. greater than 650 mG.

Passage V

In 3 studies a student investigated how the amount of water, amount of sunlight, and soil type would affect the growth of a sunflower.

Study 1

Five sunflowers *Helianthus ambiguus* (1-5) were planted outside in the same area and placed inside of containers which allowed different amounts of sunlight to enter. The student used a generic type of soil and watered each plant three times a day with 20 mL of water. The sunflowers were tended to over the course of 60 days. At the conclusion of the 60 days the student measured the height of each sunflower. She recorded her results in Table 1.

Table 1		
Sunflower	Amount of sunlight (%)	Final height (cm)
1	0%	15
2	25%	22
3	50%	39
4	75%	52
5	100%	80

Study 2

The student planted five *Helianthus ambiguus* outside in the same area. A generic type of soil was used and the plants were watered three times a day, for 60 days, with a different amount of water. At the conclusion of the 60 days the student measured the height of each sunflower. She recorded her results in Table 2.

Table 2		
Sunflower	Amount of water per day (mL)	Final height (cm)
1	0 mL	48
2	10 mL	55
3	20 mL	80
4	30 mL	87
5	40 mL	102

Study 3

The student planted five *Helianthus ambiguus* outside in five different areas, each with a different type of the soil. The nutrient composition of the soils varied. The student watered each plant three times a day, for 60 days, each with 20 mL of water. At the conclusion of the 60 days the student measured the height of each sunflower. She recorded her results in Table 3.

Table 3		
Sunflower	Soil type	Final height (cm)
1	A	98
2	B	80
3	C	57
4	D	42
5	E	33

27. According to the results of Study 1, as the amount of sunlight given to the sunflowers increased, the final height of each sunflower:
    A. increased only.
    B. decreased only.
    C. remained constant.
    D. varied, with no general trend.

28. According to the results of Study 2, as the amount of water per day given to the sunflowers increased, the final height of each sunflower:
    F. increased only.
    G. decreased only.
    H. increased, then decreased.
    J. decreased, then increased.

29. Suppose the student wanted to plot a graph with the sunflower number on the x-axis and the final height on the y-xis. Suppose a best-fit line was drawn. Based on Study 3, the slope of this line would be best described as:
    A. a positive slope.
    B. a negative slope.
    C. a slope of 0.
    D. no slope.

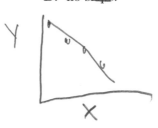

30. The student desired to grow an additional sunflower to approximately 66 cm. Based on the results of Studies 1 and 2, the amount of sunlight and amount of water per day, respectively, that the student should give the plant would be:

F. 20 % and 10 mL.

G. 20 % and 15 mL.

H. 80 % and 10 mL.

J. 80 % and 15 mL.

31. Suppose a sixth sunflower was tested in Study 1. Based on Table 1, if the amount of sunlight given to this sunflower was 40%, the final height, approximately, would be:

A. 17 cm.

B. 30 cm.

C. 45 cm.

D. 71 cm.

20 mL

32. Based on the results of the studies, which sunflower finished with a final height of approximately 1 *meter*?

F. Sunflower 1 in Study 1

G. Sunflower 5 in Study 2

H. Sunflower 2 in Study 3

J. Sunflower 5 in Study 3

33. Based on Tables 1-3, which soil type was used in Studies 1 and 2?

A. Soil type A

B. Soil type B

C. Soil type C

D. Soil type D

Passage VI

Three students performed an experiment to determine the rate at which four spherically shaped metal balls cooled in a freezer.

Each of the four balls were fitted with a thermocouple to measure the core temperature. Then, the four balls were set to different temperatures and the students placed them in a freezer set to 0°C at time = 0 min (see Figure 1).

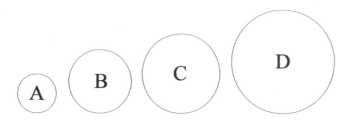

Figure 1

The students measured various physical properties of the four balls to help them better understand their cooling properties. Their results are shown in Table 1.

Table 1			
Ball	Mass (kg)	Volume (cm³)	Surface Area (cm²)
A	2.0	4.0	9.2
B	5.5	8.0	18.7
C	8.9	12.0	26.3
D	14.3	16.0	41.8

The balls were allowed to cool over the next 12 min while the temperature of the freezer was kept constant at 0°C. The students constructed a graph of the temperature of each ball over the 12 min cooling period. These results are shown in Figure 2. For each ball, the *cooling rate* at a given time is defined as the slope of the graph at that time.

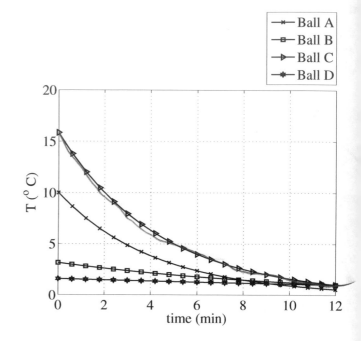

Figure 2

34. Based on the results of the experiment, as the mass of the ball increased, the volume:
    F. increased only.
    G. decreased only.
    H. remained constant.
    J. varied, with no general trend.

35. Based on the results of the experiment, as the mass of the ball increased, the surface area:
    A. increased only.
    B. decreased only.
    C. remained constant.
    D. varied, with no general trend.

36. Based on the results of the experiment, for a given ball, as the time the ball was in the freezer increased, the temperature of the ball:

    F. increased only.
    G. decreased only.
    H. remained constant.
    J. varied, with no general trend.

37. Suppose an additional ball was introduced into the experiment. According to Table 1, if the mass of the ball was measured to be 3.1 kg, the volume of the ball would be closest to which of the following?

    A. 3.1 cm^3
    B. 4.8 cm^3
    C. 11.1 cm^3
    D. 13.6 cm^3

38. Based on Figure 2, the cooling rate of Ball C, if it were measured, would have which of the following units?

    F. min/kg
    G. cm^3/kg
    H. cm^3/min
    J. °C/min

39. Suppose the experiment was allowed to continue for an additional 10 minutes. Based on the passage, the temperature of Ball C measured at that time would be closest to which of the following?

    A. -2°C
    B. 0°C
    C. 2°C
    D. 5°C

40. Suppose an additional 2.0 kg *plastic* ball was introduced into the experiment. Based on the data and other information provided, how would using plastic, instead of metal, change the results of the experiment?

    F. The cooling rate of the 2.0 kg plastic ball would be higher than the 2.0 kg metal ball.
    G. The cooling rate of the 2.0 kg plastic ball would be lower than the 2.0 kg metal ball.
    H. The cooling rate of the 2.0 kg plastic ball would be the same as the 2.0 kg metal ball.
    J. Cannot be determined from the given information.

CHAPTER 2

ADVANCED QUESTIONS TYPES

2.1 Yes, Yes, No, No

> " *The only source of knowledge is experience.* " — ALBERT EINSTEIN

Welcome to the next step in your journey towards properly tackling the ACT science section! In this chapter we will be introducing more advanced question types and adding new layers to your already expanding repertoire. These types of questions comprise approximately 5-10% of the science section. That may not seem like much, but the experience you will gain in this chapter can make the difference between the score you really want and the score you kind of want.

We will begin with a unique question type, the **Yes, Yes, No, No**. These questions are very popular throughout the ACT science section, so you are likely to spot a few in any set of 40 questions. Let us begin with an example.

YES, YES, NO, NO EXAMPLE 1

Table 1	
Contestant	Time to finish race (min)
Tortoise	11.8
Hare	12.2

QUESTION

1. An expert predicted that the hare would finish the race first. Does Table 1 support this claim?
    A. Yes; The tortoise finished with a faster time than the hare.
    B. Yes; The tortoise finished with a slower time than the hare.
    C. No; The tortoise finished with a faster time than the hare.
    D. No; The tortoise finished with a slower time than the hare.

You were probably able to answer the above question without a special tactic. However, the approach we are going to use will help you, at the very least, whittle these question types down to two answers and give you a clearer picture as to which answer choice is correct. Each answer choice consists of two parts – the answer and the explanation. The explanation are facts and easier to check, while the yes/no part takes more thought. You should *NOT* try to figure out whether the answer is Yes or No first. Instead, look at the second half, or explanation, of each answer choice to verify whether or not the fact is supported by the data.

Looking at the above example we can see that the tortoise finishes with a faster time than the hare. Based on their explanations, the correct answer must then be answer choice A or C. Next, we use our reasoning skills to determine if the correct explanation, "*The tortoise finished with a faster time than the hare*" agrees or disagrees with the question. In this case the explanation disagrees with the prediction. Answer choice C is correct.

Verifying the explanations is always an efficient way to eliminate incorrect answer choices. In some cases, the explanations of three answer choices are incorrect, leaving only the correct answer choice even before you've verified the Yes or No.

Lastly, the answer choices need not say Yes, Yes, No, No for this skill to apply. Whenever you see a comparison between two items, each with two different explanations, you should fall back on this strategy.

Your Objective: Revisit these figures shown in Chapter One and answer the following questions using the Yes, Yes, No, No skill.

YES, YES, NO, NO EXAMPLE 2

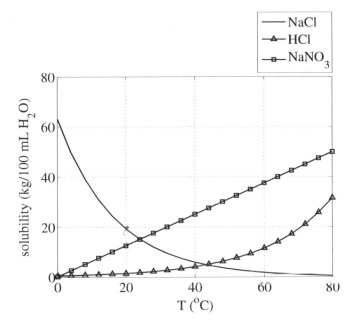

Figure 1

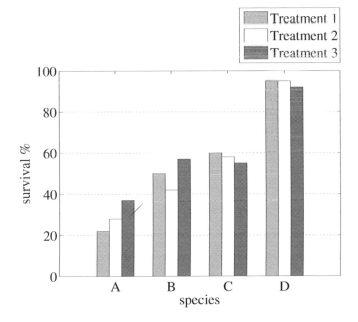

Figure 2

QUESTIONS

2. A chemist claimed that NaCl would have the highest solubility at 20°C. Does Figure 1 support this claim?
   F. Yes, because at 20°C NaCl has the lowest solubility among the three compounds.
   G. No, because 20°C NaCl has the lowest solubility among the three compounds.
   H. Yes, because 20°C NaCl has the highest solubility among the three compounds.
   J. No, because 20°C NaCl has the highest solubility among the three compounds.

3. A chemist claimed that HCl would have the highest solubility at 40°C. Does Figure 1 support this claim?
   A. Yes, because at 40°C HCl has the lowest solubility among the three compounds.
   B. No, because at 40°C HCl has the lowest solubility among the three compounds.
   C. Yes, because at 40°C HCl has the highest solubility among the three compounds.
   D. No, because at 40°C HCl has the highest solubility among the three compounds.

4. A biologist predicted Treatment 3 would yield the highest survival percentage for species D. Does Figure 2 support this claim?
   F. Yes; Species D exhibited the highest survival percentage when exposed to Treatment 3.
   G. Yes; Species D exhibited the lowest survival percentage when exposed to Treatment 3.
   H. No; Species D exhibited the highest survival percentage when exposed to Treatment 3.
   J. No; Species D exhibited the lowest survival percentage when exposed to Treatment 3.

5. For a specific experiment, a survival percentage less than 40% is required. After analyzing the results of the experiment, which species should be chosen for the experiment?
   A. Species A, because the survival percentage was lower than 40% for all treatments.
   B. Species B, because the survival percentage was lower than 40% for all treatments.
   C. Species A, because the survival percentage was higher than 40% for all treatments.
   D. Species B, because the survival percentage was higher than 40% for all treatments.

2.2   Cannot Be Determined

> " *If your answer is not there, that's the answer.* "

The **cannot be determined** answer choice tends to distract students. When you see this as a possible answer choice, do not change your approach. Search for your locators; if you fail to find them, you can be confident in choosing cannot be determined as the correct answer.

Your Objective: Answer the following questions by determining whether or not you can locate the correct answer. If you can, do so. If not, choose cannot be determined.

CANNOT BE DETERMINED EXAMPLE 1

Study 1

829 people were placed into four different groups: A, B, C and D. Each group was given the same task to complete in 60 minutes. The completion percentages of the four groups are shown in Figure 1.

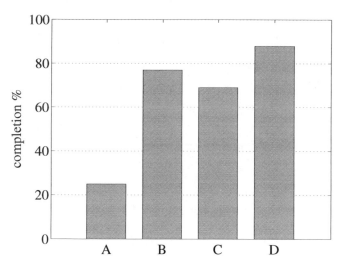

Figure 1

Study 2

The same 829 people were shuffled into different groups and asked to repeat the task from Study 1. The results are tabulated below.

Table 1		
Group	Number of people	Completion (%)
A	140	89
B	327	93
C	255	91
D	107	90

QUESTIONS

6. According to Study 1, the greatest amount of people were assigned to which group?
   F. Group B
   G. Group C
   H. Group D
   J. Cannot be determined from the given information.

7. According to Study 2, the greatest amount of people were assigned to which group?
   A. Cannot be determined from the given information.
   B. Group B
   C. Group C
   D. Group D

8. Based on Studies 1 and 2, did completing the task a second time improve the completion percentages of the groups?
   F. Yes; The completion percentages of Study 1 are generally higher than those of Study 2.
   G. Yes; The completion percentages of Study 2 are generally higher than those of Study 1.
   H. No; The completion percentages of Study 1 are generally higher than those of Study 2.
   J. No; The data is insufficient.

9. Suppose the 829 people consisted of ages 17-23. Based on the passage, how would this information change the results, if at all?
   A. The completion percentages would be higher.
   B. The completion percentages would be lower.
   C. The results of the study would not change.
   D. Cannot be determined from the given information.

2.3 Equations as Answer Choices

"
Pick a point and plug it in.
"

When **equations appear as answer choices**, pick a point on the figure or a row on the table and plug those values into the answer choices. Remember to use your estimation skills to avoid challenging math calculations. For more complex questions, the passage can hold a clue as to which numbers to plug in. This, of course, is assuming the question directs you to the passage with a first locator. Furthermore, solving these types of questions correctly can sometimes help you answer extrapolation questions later in the passage. Let's look at an example together.

Your Objective: Complete the following questions by plugging values into the answer choices. Some questions may be easily solved using the correct answers of preceding questions.

EQUATIONS AS ANSWER CHOICES EXAMPLE 1

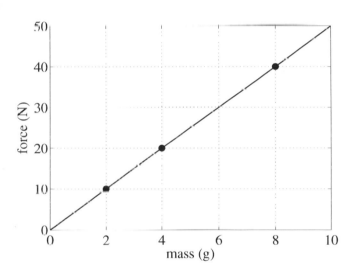

Figure 1

Table 1	
Time (sec)	Speed (m/sec)
0	0
1.00	3.00
2.00	6.00
4.00	12.00
8.00	24.00

QUESTIONS

10. According to Figure 1, the results of the experiment are best modeled by which equation?
    - **F.** mass (g) = 0.2 × force (N)
    - **G.** mass (g) = 5.0 × force (N)
    - **H.** force (N) = 0.2 × mass (g)
    - **J.** force (N) = 5.0 × mass (g)

11. Suppose an object with a mass of 14 g was tested. Based on Figure 1, the force of this object would be which of the following?
    - **A.** 50 N
    - **B.** 60 N
    - **C.** 70 N
    - **D.** 80 N

12. According to Table 1, the results of the experiment are best modeled by which equation?
    - **F.** time (s) = 2.0 × speed (m/s)
    - **G.** time (s) = 3.0 × speed (m/s)
    - **H.** speed (m/s) = 2.0 × time (s)
    - **J.** speed (m/s) = 3.0 × time (s)

13. Suppose an additional time of 15 sec was added to Table 1. Based on Table 1, a time of 15 sec would equate to which speed?
    - **A.** 30 m/s
    - **B.** 35 m/s
    - **C.** 40 m/s
    - **D.** 45 m/s

2.4   Mixing

" *Do not add the points, pick the number in the middle.* "

Mixing problems, if they do pop up, tend to be the last question of a passage. Whenever you see the words mix or mixing, you must be keen on taking the average of the two data points you will be required to locate. A common mistake is to choose the answer choice that represents the sum of the two points. The idea is that, typically, the question refers to a concentration of a solution. Mixing two different concentrations results in a new concentration that is somewhere in the middle of the original two. For example: Mixing lightly salted water and heavily salted water does not yield even more heavily salted water. The result is somewhere between lightly and heavily salted.

Your Objective: Answer the following mixing questions.

MIXING EXAMPLE 1

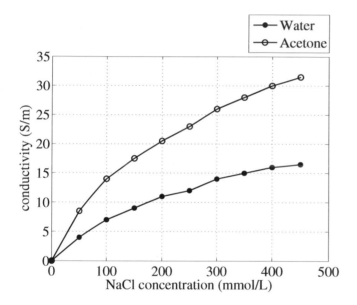

Figure 1

QUESTIONS

14. Suppose that 5 mL of a 100 mmol/L NaCl-water solution is mixed with 5 mL of a 200 mmol/L NaCl-water solution. According to Figure 1, the conductivity of the resulting solution will be closest to which of the following?
    F.   7 S/m
    G.   9 S/m
    H.   11 S/m
    J.   18 S/m

15. Suppose that 20 mL of a 100 mmol/L NaCl-acetone solution is mixed with 20 mL of a 300 mmol/L NaCl-acetone solution. According to Figure 1, the conductivity of the resulting solution will be closest to which of the following?
    A.   14 S/m
    B.   20 S/m
    C.   25 S/m
    D.   40 S/m

16. Suppose that 50 mL of a 200 mmol/L NaCl-water solution is mixed with 50 mL of a 200 mmol/L NaCl-acetone solution. According to Figure 1, the conductivity of the resulting solution will be closest to which of the following?
    F.   9 S/m
    G.   11 S/m
    H.   16 S/m
    J.   20 S/m

2.5 Scatter Plots

Scatter plots are very popular on the ACT Science section. Knowing how to properly read a scatter plot will help you better locate correct answers. On a scatter plot, each point represents data that the experimenter obtained while conducting the experiment. You will also notice a line of best-fit going through the pattern of points. Questions dealing with scatter plots require you to find how often the experimenter obtained results. You can find your answer by identifying the time axis and then counting how frequently the points are plotted on the figure. **Ignore** the part of the question that asks how the data was obtained. This information will not help you answer these types of questions.

Your Objective: Answer the following scatter plot questions.

SCATTER PLOT EXAMPLE 1

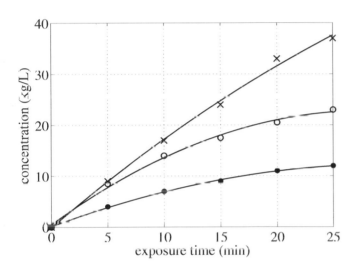

Figure 1

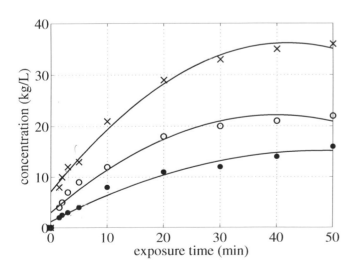

Figure 2

QUESTIONS

17. According to Figure 1, from 0 min until 25 min, how often was the sample removed from the device for analysis?
    A. Every 0.5 min
    B. Every 1.0 min
    C. Every 5.0 min
    D. Every 8.0 min

18. According to Figure 1, if an additional 5 minutes had been added to the experiment, the concentration of all three trials would most likely have:
    F. increased.
    G. decreased.
    H. remained constant.
    J. varied, with no general trend.

19. According to Figure 2, from 0 min until 5 min, how often was the specimen cut and placed into the device for testing?
    A. Every 1.0 min
    B. Every 5.0 min
    C. Every 10.0 min
    D. The frequency of the plots is not constant.

20. According to Figure 2, from 10 min until 50 min, how often was the specimen cut and placed into the device for testing?
    F. Every 1.0 min
    G. Every 5.0 min
    H. Every 10.0 min
    J. Every 15.0 min

2.6   Water and Drying

A lot of science experiments in the world deal with the properties of water and how it behaves with other compounds. The ACT Science section mimics this pattern and many answer choices deal directly with the properties of water, specifically the boiling point of water: $100°C$. These questions do not always give specific locators and require a bit of outside knowledge. To best prepare for these questions, we want you to anticipate water, moisture, or boiling water as the correct answers.

Your Objective: Answer the following questions based on your knowledge of water.

WATER AND DRYING EXAMPLE

Experiment 1

Before the salt mixtures were administered a drying agent was placed in each tank and allowed to sit for two days. Then, 3 salt mixtures were made with water and stirred in separate tanks. Several properties were measured and the results organized in Table 1.

Table 1			
Tank	Salt in mixture	$\Delta T(°C)$	Relative Humidity (%)
1	NaCl	5.9	15.8
2	$MgCl_2$	6.2	17.2
3	KOH	6.8	18.1

QUESTIONS

21. Suppose an additional salt was tested that yielded a ΔT value of $7.5°C$. The relative humidity of this additional salt would most likely be closest to which of the following?
    A. 15.5%
    B. 16.3%
    C. 17.6%
    D. 18.8%

22. What was the purpose of allowing the mixtures to sit for two days before recording the results in Experiment 1?
    F. To ensure the relative humidity of each salt mixture in each tank was constant
    G. To ensure the temperature of each tank was constant
    H. To remove any H_2O present in the tanks
    J. To remove any salts present in the tanks

The questions below do not refer to any set of data.

23. In all 3 studies, the purpose of oven-drying the medium was to remove the:
    A. organic matter.
    B. salts.
    C. electrostatic force.
    D. moisture.

24. What was the most likely reason the scientist kept the wet soil in a heater, set to $105°C$, for 1 hour before beginning the experiment?
    F. To remove the moisture.
    G. To remove any organic matter in the soil.
    H. To ensure the soil was room temperature.
    J. To thoroughly clean the soil of unwanted contaminants.

2.7 Chapter Test: Advanced Question Types

This next chapter test will focus on the basics from Chapter One and the advanced questions presented in Chapter Two. As you did with the first chapter test, time yourself and aim to finish the test in the prescribed 35 minutes or within your timing accommodation. This test will feel a bit tougher than the previous one since we are adding more types of questions. Do your best to stay focused and remember what you've learned from Chapter Two.

The most important thing to remember, and we will remind you of this each time, is to use the proper mindset and to rely on the tactics. Answering questions by solely relying on your science knowledge will hurt your progression as you move forward. Stick to your locators to start your thought process so you develop a flexible approach.

Good luck!

SCIENCE
35 Minutes—40 Questions

DIRECTIONS: There are six passages in this test. Each passage is followed by several questions. After reading a passage, choose the best answer to each question and fill in the corresponding oval on your answer document. You may refer to the passages as often as necessary.

You are NOT permitted to use a calculator on this test.

Passage I

Respiration rates were studied for two different types of bacteria: *aerobic bacteria* and *E. coli* (an anaerobic bacterium). When aerobic bacteria undergo respiration, O_2 is consumed and CO_2 is produced. When *E. coli* undergo respiration, NO_3^- is consumed and NO_2^- is produced.

Study

At the start of spring, 3 soil sections — each 1.0 m long, 1.0 m wide, and 3.0 m deep — were removed from the surface of two different sources. Both sources are known to contain aerobic bacteria and *E. coli*. Each soil section was placed in a different tank made entirely of glass to allow sunlight to penetrate. Gas emissions were measured using an available instrument and the tanks were left outside near their respective sources.

Gas emissions were measured, in mol/cm^3, once a month for 3 months. The temperature inside of each tank equaled the temperature of its respective source at all times. Water was fed to each tank through a hose at a constant rate to ensure proper respiration of the bacteria. Figure 1 shows the total emission of CO_2 and NO_2^- from Source 1. Figure 2 shows the total emission of CO_2 and NO_2^- from Source 2.

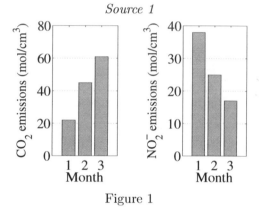

Figure 1

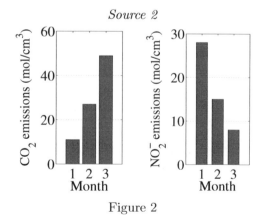

Figure 2

1. According to the results of the study, the CO_2 emissions for Source 1 each month:
   - **A.** increased only.
   - **B.** decreased only.
   - **C.** remained constant.
   - **D.** varied, with no general trend.

2. The researchers most likely chose to conduct this particular study in the spring, rather than the winter, because:
   - **F.** only aerobic bacteria undergo respiration in the spring.
   - **G.** only *E. coli* undergo respiration in the spring.
   - **H.** microorganism activity in soil is better in the spring.
   - **J.** microorganism activity in soil is better in the winter.

3. Based on the results of the study, were *E. coli* present in both sources for all 3 months?
   - **A.** Yes; CO_2 was omitted from both sources.
   - **B.** Yes; NO_2^- was emitted from both sources.
   - **C.** No; CO_2 was emitted from both sources.
   - **D.** No; NO_2^- was emitted from both sources.

4. According to Figure 1, the *total* CO_2 emissions for Source 1 is closest to which of the following?
   - **F.** 60 mol/cm^3
   - **G.** 80 mol/cm^3
   - **H.** 100 mol/cm^3
   - **J.** 120 mol/cm^3

5. Based on the study, the *volume* of each soil section is which of the following?
   - **A.** 3 m^3
   - **B.** 4 m^3
   - **C.** 5 m^3
   - **D.** 6 m^3

6. Suppose the tanks were allowed to stay near their respective source for an additional month. According to the data, the NO_2^- emissions for Source 2, in the additional month, would be closest to which of the following?
   - **F.** 5 mol/cm^3
   - **G.** 10 mol/cm^3
   - **H.** 15 mol/cm^3
   - **J.** 20 mol/cm^3

7. According to the information provided, which of the following chemical equations represents anaerobic respiration?
   - **A.** $C_6H_{12}O_6 + 6O_2 \rightarrow 6CO_2 + 6H_2O + ATP$
   - **B.** $6CO_2 + 6H_2O + ATP \rightarrow C_6H_{12}O_6 + 6O_2$
   - **C.** $2NO_2^- + O_2 \rightarrow 2NO_3^-$
   - **D.** $2NO_3^- \rightarrow 2NO_2^- + O_2$

3.1.1

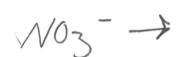

Passage II

To treat pool water for recreation, chlorine tablets can be used to kill bacteria. Chlorine breaks down into different chemicals, one of which is hypochlorous acid (HOCl). HOCl kills bacteria by attacking fats in the cell walls and destroying the enzymes inside the bacterium cell.

Two studies examined how water pH and chlorine concentration (g/mL) affected bacteria concentration (kg/L) in 25°C pool water during the summer.

Study 1

Before the start of the study, three water pools, each 40,000 liters, had pH levels set to 5, 7, and 9 using various acids and bases. Then, chlorine tablets were placed in all three water pools to yield a chlorine concentration of 75 g/mL. The bacteria concentration was measured over time using a unique device for a 50 min duration (see Figure 1).

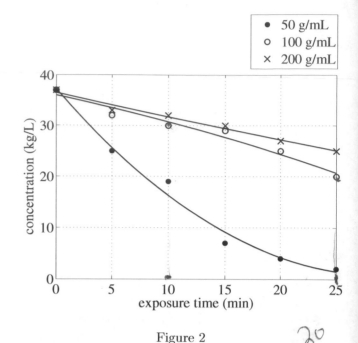

Figure 2

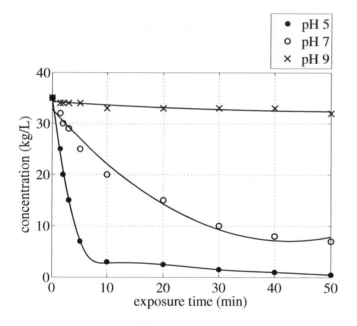

Figure 1

Study 2

Three water pools, each 40,000 liters and having a pH of 7, were subjected to different initial chlorine concentrations: 50 g/mL, 100 g/mL, and 200 g/mL. The bacteria concentration was measured using the same device from Study 1 for a 25 min duration (see Figure 2).

8. According to the results of Study 1, at 25°C and 20 min, as the pH increased the bacteria concentration:
   F. increased only.
   G. decreased only.
   H. remained constant.
   J. cannot be determined.

9. Suppose a 10 mL sample of the pool water used in Study 2 is removed at the 10 min mark for an initial chlorine concentration of 100 g/mL. Then, a second 10 mL sample is removed from the same pool at the 25 min mark. The two samples are then mixed. Which of the following is closest to the bacteria concentration of the mixture?
   A. 20 kg/L
   B. 25 kg/L
   C. 30 kg/L
   D. 35 kg/L

10. According to Figure 2, from 0 min until 25 min, how often was the bacteria concentration measured using the device?
    F. Every 1 min
    G. Every 2 min
    H. Every 5 min
    J. Every 10 min

11. Which variable did not have the same value in Study 1, but did have the same value in Study 2?
    A. pH
    B. Water temperature (°C)
    C. Chlorine concentration (g/mL)
    D. Bacteria concentration (kg/L)

12. A student hypothesized that as the initial concentration of chlorine increased, the bacteria concentration at a given time would decrease. Do the results of the study support this hypothesis?
    F. Yes; At a given time, as the initial concentration of chlorine increased the bacteria concentration increased.
    G. No; At a given time, as the initial concentration of chlorine increased the bacteria concentration increased.
    H. Yes; At a given time, as the initial concentration of chlorine decreased the bacteria concentration increased.
    J. No; At a given time, as the initial concentration of chlorine decreased the bacteria concentration increased.

13. Suppose the pool water was kept constant at a temperature of 30°C. How would this change affect the results of the study?
    A. The bacteria concentrations for all three pools would be higher.
    B. The bacteria concentration for all three pools would be lower.
    C. The bacteria concentration for all three pools would be similar to the current study.
    D. The information given is insufficient to determine a change in the results.

14. A researcher stated that a more *acidic* water would be better for eliminating bacteria. Do the results of Study 1 support this claim?
    F. Yes; The acidic water sample resulted in a higher bacteria concentration at all times.
    G. Yes; The basic water sample resulted in a higher bacteria concentration at all times.
    H. No; The acidic water sample resulted in a higher bacteria concentration at all times.
    J. No; The basic water sample resulted in a higher bacteria concentration at all times.

Passage III

An ideal gas is a theoretical gas that behaves according to the ideal gas law. It is composed of randomly moving particles that avoid one another, except for elastic collisions. The *compressability factor* (z) is a value that determines the deviation of a real gas from ideal behavior and is defined by the following equation:

$$z = \frac{\text{Actual volume of real gas}}{\text{Ideal volume of gas}}$$

Figure 1 shows how the compressability factor varies with pressure for 5 real gases at 298 K. Figure 2 shows how the compressability factor varies with temperature for 5 real gases at 1 atm.

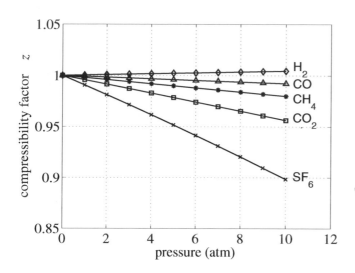

Figure 1

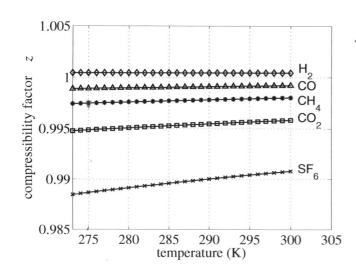

Figure 2

15. According to Figure 2, at 275 K, the value of z for CH_4 is approximately:
   A. 0.9925.
   B. 0.9950.
   C. 0.9975.
   D. 1.0000.

16. According to Figure 1, for CO_2, as pressure increases the compressability factor:
   F. increases only.
   G. decreases only.
   H. remains constant.
   J. varies, but with no general trend.

17. A student attempted to find a best-fit linear approximation for compressability factor versus pressure for SF_6. Which of the following best models this approximation?
   A. $z = -0.01 \times$ pressure (atm) $+ 1$
   B. $z = 0.01 \times$ pressure (atm) $+ 1$
   C. pressure (atm) $= -0.01 \times z + 1$
   D. pressure (atm) $= 0.01 \times z + 1$

18. An ideal gas has a constant compressability factor of 1. Among the gases tested, a chemist hypothesized that CO_2 would deviate most from ideal behavior. Does Figure 1 agree with this claim?
   F. Yes; Among the gases tested, CO_2 deviated most from ideal behavior.
   G. Yes; Among the gases tested, SF_6 deviated most from ideal behavior.
   H. No; Among the gases tested, CO_2 deviated most from ideal behavior.
   J. No; Among the gases tested, SF_6 deviated most from ideal behavior.

19. Suppose the data for z had been generated at 273 K instead of 298 K for Figure 1. Based on Figures 1 and 2, the value of z at 273 K, compared to 298 K, would be:
   A. lower for most gases tested.
   B. higher for most gases tested.
   C. identical for all gases tested.
   D. unable to be determined.

20. Based on the passage, which real gas has an actual volume greater than its ideal gas volume at 10 atm?
   F. H_2
   G. CO
   H. CH_4
   J. CO_2

Passage IV

Radioactive decay is a process that depends on the instability of a particular atom. When a radioactive isotope undergoes radioactive decay, the atom transmutates into a different atom. The *half-life*, $T_{1/2}$, is the amount of time it takes for half of the initial number of atoms to decay. It is calculated using the following equation:

$$T_{1/2} = 0.7\tau$$

where τ represents the mean lifetime of the radioisotope. Table 1 gives the value of $T_{1/2}$ (in yr) for 7 different radioisotopes.

Table 1		
Element	Isotope	$T_{1/2}$ (yr)
Carbon	C-14	5,715
Plutonium	Pu-239	2.4×10^4
Uranium	U-233	1.6×10^5
Technetium	Tc-99	2.1×10^5
Uranium	U-235	7.0×10^8
Uranium	U-238	4.5×10^9
Thorium	Th-232	1.4×10^{10}

Figure 1 shows, for each of 5 isotopes listed in Table 1, the number of atoms, N, versus time (in 10^8 yr) for a sample initially containing 1,000 atoms.

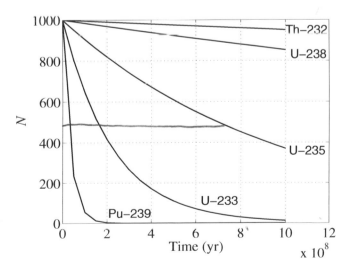

Figure 1

21. Suppose a sample contained 500 U-235 atoms at time = 0. Based on Table 1, how much time will have elapsed when 250 U-235 atoms remain?
    A. 3×10^8 yr
    B. 5×10^8 yr
    C. 7×10^8 yr
    D. 9×10^8 yr

22. A scientist guessed that Plutonium-239 would have a longer half-life than Technetium-99. Does Table 1 support this claim?
    F. Yes; Plutonium-239 has a longer half-life than Technetium-99.
    G. Yes; Technetium-99 has a longer half-life than Plutonium-239.
    H. No; Plutonium-239 has a longer half-life than Technetium-99.
    J. No; Technetium-99 has a longer half-life than Plutonium-239.

23. According to Figure 1, how long did it take for 150 Uranium-238 atoms to decay?
    A. 10 yr
    B. 7.0×10^8 yr
    C. 10×10^8 yr
    D. 4.5×10^9 yr

24. According to Figure 1, at 12×10^8 years, approximately how many Uranium-235 atoms will remain?
    F. 300 atoms
    G. 400 atoms
    H. 500 atoms
    J. 600 atoms

25. Based on Table 1 and Figure 1, if a sample initially contains 1,000 Tc-99 atoms, how many atoms would remain after 4×10^8 years?
    A. less than 180 atoms
    B. between 180 and 700 atoms
    C. between 700 and 900 atoms
    D. more than 900 atoms

26. Based on the passage and Table 1, the mean lifetime, τ, for Carbon-14 is closest to which of the following?
    F. 3,707 yr
    G. 5,470 yr
    H. 5,715 yr
    J. 8,150 yr

Passage V

Two college students decided to perform an experiment to test the different components of cars and the effect the components have on travel time.

Study 1

Five cars were placed on a $^1/_4$-mile straight track. Each car had the same 750 ft^3/min (cfm) *supercharger* and 450 *horsepower* (hp) engine. The weights of the cars were documented. One student stood by and measured the time it took for the other student to accelerate from rest with each car and travel the $^1/_4$-mile track. The students recorded their data in Table 1.

Table 1		
Car	Weight (kg)	$^1/_4$-mile time (s)
A	1,814	10
B	1,886	10.6
C	1,619	9.3
D	1,675	9.8
E	2,013	12.3

Study 2

One of the five cars from Study 1 was selected. The supercharger component of the car was altered five different times. One student stood by and measured the time it took for the other student to accelerate from rest and travel the $^1/_4$-mile track. The students recorded their data in Table 2.

Table 2		
Trial	Supercharger (cfm)	$^1/_4$-mile time (s)
1	750	12.3
2	825	12.0
3	900	11.6
4	1,000	11.2
5	1,050	10.9

Study 3

One of the five cars from Study 1 was selected. The engine horsepower component of the car was altered five different times. One student stood by and measured the time it took for the other student to accelerate from rest and travel the $^1/_4$-mile track. The students recorded their data in Table 3.

Table 3		
Trial	Engine horsepower (hp)	$^1/_4$-mile time (s)
1	350	10.2
2	400	9.7
3	450	9.3
4	500	8.9
5	550	8.4

27. According to Table 1, as the weight of the car increased, the $^1/_4$-mile time:
    A. increased only.
    B. decreased only.
    C. increased, then decreased.
    D. decreased, then increased.

28. Before the study, one of the students hypothesized that the car with the lightest mass would yield the fastest time. Do the results of Study 1 support this claim?
    F. Yes; Car E had the lightest mass and yielded the slowest time.
    G. Yes; Car C had the lightest mass and yielded the fastest time.
    H. No; Car C had the lightest mass and yielded the slowest time.
    J. No; Car E had the lightest mass and yielded the fastest time.

29. Suppose an additional trial had been tested with a 950 cfm supercharger. Based on the results of Study 2, the $^1/_4$-mile time would most likely be closest to which of the following?
    A. 11.2 cfm
    B. 11.4 cfm
    C. 11.6 cfm
    D. 11.8 cfm

30. Based on Studies 1 and 2, which car was used in Study 2?

   F. Car A

   G. Car B

   H. Car E

   J. Cannot be determined from the given information

31. Which variable had the same value throughout Study 1, but did not have the same value throughout Study 3?

   A. Weight (kg)

   B. $^1/_4$-mile time (s)

   C. Supercharger (cfm)

   D. Engine horsepower (hp)

32. Based on Studies 1 and 3, which car was used in Study 3?

   F. Car A

   G. Car B

   H. Car C

   J. Cannot be determined from the given information

33. Suppose the procedure in Study 1 for Car E had been repeated, except with a 300 hp engine instead of a 450 hp engine. Based on the results of Studies 1 and 2, the $^1/_4$-mile time would most likely have been:

   A. less than 9.8 s.

   B. between 9.8 s and 10.6 s.

   C. between 10.6 s and 12.3 s.

   D. greater than 12.3 s.

Passage VI

Water pollution occurs when pollutants are discharged into bodies of water. Numerous water treatments are available to cleanse water bodies of unnecessary pollutants. A researcher conducted an experiment to test the effectiveness of certain water treatments against unwanted bacteria.

Experiment 1

Four 100 mL samples of clean water at 25°C were each subjected to a different unknown strain of bacteria (A-D). A measuring device was connected to a computer to calculate the survival percentage of the bacteria. A water cleanser was placed in each sample and allowed to sit for 1 day. At the same time the next day, the survival percentage of the bacteria was measured. The experiment was repeated for three different water treatements (see Figure 1). The different pH values of the water treatments are shown in Table 1.

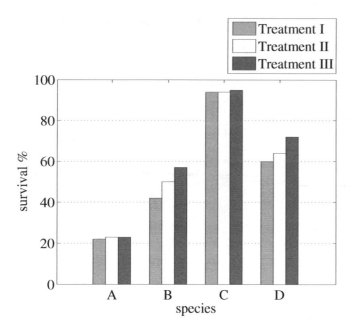

Figure 1

Table 1	
Water treatment	pH level
I	5
II	7
III	10

Experiment 2

Four 100 mL samples of water containing one of the bacteria species from Experiment 1 were collected. The temperatures of the water samples were adjusted. A measuring device was connected to a computer to calculate the survival percentage of the bacteria. A water cleanser was placed in each sample and allowed to sit for 1 day. At the same time the next day, the survival percentage of the bacteria was measured. The experiment was repeated for three different water treatments (see Figure 2).

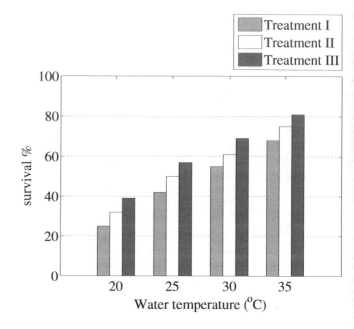

Figure 2

34. According to the results Experiment 2, for a given water treatment, as the water temperature increased the survival percentage:
- **F.** increased only.
- **G.** decreased only.
- **H.** remained constant.
- **J.** varied, but with no general trend.

35. Based on the results of Experiment 1, which bacteria species was most *resistant* to the water treatments?
- **A.** Species A
- **B.** Species B
- **C.** Species C
- **D.** Species D

36. Based on Table 1 and Figure 2, at 20°C, as the pH level of the water treatment increased, the survival percentage:

F. increased only.

G. decreased only.

H. increased, then decreased.

J. varied, but with no general trend.

37. Which variable had the same value throughout Experiment 1, but did not have the same value throughout Experiment 2?

A. Bacteria species

B. Survival %

C. Water treatment

D. Water temperature (°C)

38. The researcher predicted, for a given treatment, the highest water temperature would *kill* the most bacteria. Do the results of Experiment 2 support this claim?

F. No; A water temperature of 20°C yielded the highest survival percentage.

G. No; A water temperature of 35°C yielded the highest survival percentage.

H. Yes; A water temperature of 20°C yielded the highest survival percentage.

J. Yes; A water temperature of 35°C yielded the highest survival percentage.

39. Based on the results of the experiments, which bacteria species was used in Experiment 2?

A. Species A

B. Species B

C. Species C

D. Species D

40. Suppose an additional species, Species E, had yielded a survival percentage of 60% at 25°C with Treatment II. According to the results of the experiments, if the researcher wanted to promote the growth of Species E, the researcher would use:

F. colder water, because as water temperature decreases survival percentage decreases.

G. warmer water, because as water temperature decreases survival percentage decreases.

H. colder water, because as water temperature increases survival percentage decreases.

J. warmer water, because as water temperature increases survival percentage decreases.

CHAPTER 3

SCIENTIFIC METHOD

3.1 The Elements of an Experiment

> " *What you change, what you measure, everything else is constant.* "

This chapter focuses on helping you better understand the experiments...**without reading any of the text**. There are certainly some questions that require you to find specific locators in the passage. But scientific method questions require you to be able to extract the different elements of the experiments efficiently. The text, most times, will distract you.

ELEMENT	TABLE LOCATION	FIGURE LOCATION	HOW TO REMEMBER IT
Independent variable	Left-most column(s)	X-axis, Legend	"What you change"
Dependent variable	Right-most column(s)	Y-axis	"What you measure"
Constants	Not there	Not there	"Everything else"
Control group	n/a	n/a	"Basis of comparison"

Your Objective: Let me walk you through an example analyzing the table below.

Sample	Sun	Soil	Water (mL)	Height (cm)
1	20%	A	100	20.1
2	40%	A	100	23.7
3	60%	A	100	27.5
4	20%	A	100	20.1
5	20%	B	100	17.2
6	20%	C	100	15.8
7	20%	A	100	20.1
8	20%	A	150	22.9
9	20%	A	200	25.3

First, look at samples 1-3. Notice that the amount of sun is changing, the soil is constant, the water is constant, and the height is being measured. We can distinguish between the sun being **changed** and the height being **measured** because the sun is to the left (independent variable) and the height is to the right (dependent variable). Another way to tell the difference is the sun is being changed to pretty round numbers and the height is measured with ugly decimals. If you were to conduct an experiment, you would purposely change to pretty round numbers (independent variable) and you would measure ugly numbers (dependent variable).

Now, look at samples 4-6. Notice the sun is now constant and the soil is being changed. In science you are only allowed to change one variable at a time. We cannot change the sun and the soil simultaneously because then we will not know which variable is causing the height to fluctuate. The independent variable is now the soil and the dependent variable is still the height. It is common for the dependent variable to be the same for different studies.

We did all of this **without needing any text!** You can do the same for samples 7-9.

Your Objective: Answer the questions below using the same table.

Scientific Method Example 1

Sample	Sun	Soil	Water (mL)	Height (cm)
1	20%	A	100	20.1
2	40%	A	100	23.7
3	60%	A	100	27.5
4	20%	A	100	20.1
5	20%	B	100	17.2
6	20%	C	100	15.8
7	20%	A	100	20.1
8	20%	A	150	22.9
9	20%	A	200	25.3

Questions

1. Based on Samples 7-9, which element represents the independent variable?
   A. Sun
   B. Soil
   C. Water (mL)
   D. Height (cm)

2. Based on Samples 7-9, which element represents the dependent variable?
   F. Sun
   G. Soil
   H. Water (mL)
   J. Height (cm)

3. Based on Samples 7-9, which element(s) represent constants? (more than one answer may be correct)
   A. Sun
   B. Soil
   C. Water (mL)
   D. Height (cm)

Your Objective: Let me walk you through an example analyzing the figure below.

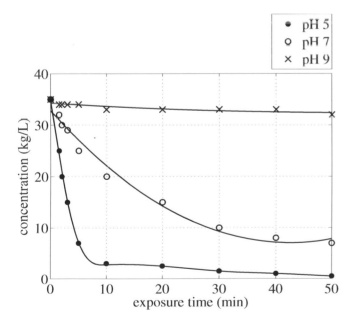

First, look at the legend (pH) and the x-axis (time). Both can be considered independent variables because they are both being purposely changed. However, when you see time as your x axis, we want to ignore it. For the purpose of taking this test it is not optimal for us to think of time as our independent variable. When looking at this figure, understand that *pH* is the variable being purposely changed and *concentration* (kg/L) is being measured.

Do you notice any other variables besides pH, exposure time, and concentration? How about water temperature? Or air pressure? No? If you are looking for additional variables because of a locator in a question and the locator directs you to a figure where you cannot find those variables, then you know they are **constants**. We can look at the figure to the left and deduce that anything besides pH, exposure time, and concentration, is constant...**without needing any text yet again!**

So, when you look at a figure, find what is being changed, what is being measured, and then understand that everything else is constant.

Your Objective: Answer the scientific method questions concerning the figure below.

SCIENTIFIC METHOD EXAMPLE 2

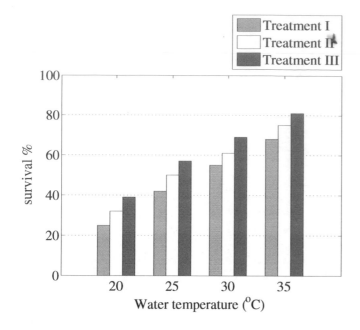

QUESTIONS

4. Based on the figure, which element represents an independent variable?
   F. Water temperature (°C)
   G. survival %
   H. Air humidity
   J. Air pressure

5. Based on the figure, which element represents a dependent variable?
   A. Water temperature (°C)
   B. survival %
   C. Treatment type
   D. Air pressure

6. Based on the figure, which element represents a constant?
   F. Water temperature (°C)
   G. survival %
   H. Treatment type
   J. Air pressure

The **control group** is best identified from experience. A good way to define a control group is it's the *basis of comparison*. Let's say you are changing the amount of water you give plants and measuring their growth. In order to compare the growth properly you need to have one plant that does not receive any water. That is your control group. Essentially, it is the trial in the experiment that is just being left alone. If you genetically change a tomato...you need a normal tomato. If you plant different types of enhanced fertilizer in fields...you need a field with normal fertilizer. Let's get more comfortable with experiments by coming up with our own!

Your Objective: Create your own experiment. Try to avoid using a boring science experiment. Get creative and use one of your hobbies. We will use basketball as an example.

ELEMENT	MY EXPERIMENT	YOUR EXPERIMENT
Independent variable	Shoot from different spots on the court	
Dependent variable	Field goal %	
Constants	The person, the ball, weather	
Control group	The free-throw line shot	

CHAPTER 4

Beating the Last Questions

4.1 Inverse Trends

> *Early questions like direct trends, late questions like inverse trends.*

An inverse trend feels a bit more complex than a direct trend. After reading a figure and seeing the values increase, there is a tendency to want to pick the answer choice that also increases. This works well early on in a passage. But, as you progress towards the later quetsions, and specifically the last question, the ACT Science section tends to use inverse trends.

There are some inverse trends that you are used to identifying. For example, the faster you drive to your destination the less time it will take to get there. However, there are also a lot of inverse trends in science that you are not familiar with. These trends tend to be at the center of last questions. So, when you see a value increasing in the question, lean towards the answer choice that is decreasing. This will not work 100% of the time, but it will work the vast majority of the time. If you are certain you understand the science behind the question, then go with the answer choice you feel confident picking. However, if you get in trouble always go with the inverse trend.

Your Objective: The problems below are indicative of ones typically found as the last question of a passage.

Study 1

A student performed an experiment to measure the temperature of a beaker of water over time. The student measured 200 mL of water and placed the beaker in a freezer at -2°C. A thermometer was placed inside of the beaker and the temperature was recorded every 2 seconds (Trial 1). Then, the student measured 200 mL of water and placed the beaker on a hot plate. The hot plate was turned to 75% power. A thermometer was placed inside of the beaker and the temperature was recorded every 2 seconds (Trial 2). The student recorded the results in Figure 1.

1. Suppose that, in a new study, the student used the hot plate to heat 400 mL of water. Based on Figure 1 and other information provided, at time = 6 s, the temperature of the water inside the beaker would most likely be:
   - A. less than 5°C
   - B. between 5°C and 7.5°C
   - C. between 7.5°C and 10°C
   - D. greater than 10°C

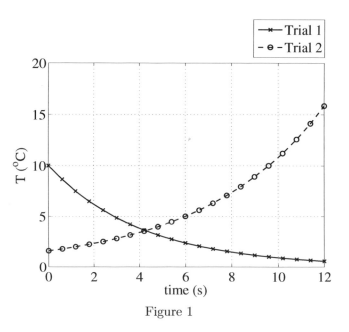

Figure 1

The questions below do not refer to any set of data.

2. As acceleration increases, will the time it takes an object to reach the bottom of an inclined plane increase or decrease, and why?
   - F. Decrease, because velocity will decrease.
   - G. Increase, because velocity will decrease.
   - H. Decrease, because velocity will increase.
   - J. Increase, because velocity will increase.

3. The LED would *best* conduct electricity if the resistance of the circuit equaled which of the following values?
   - A. 20 Ω
   - B. 30 Ω
   - C. 40 Ω
   - D. 50 Ω

4.2 Anticipating the Extra Step

> " *Logic is the beginning of wisdom, not the end.* " — Leonard Nimoy

Last questions have a certain logic to them. Typically they require exactly two steps. The first step is relatively easy. For example, finding a value on a figure or table. The second step requires a bit more work. For example, applying an inverse trend from a different study to the value in the first step. However, we can skip this second step by thinking about the structure of the answer choices. Sometimes your initial value splits the answer choices into two groups: answer choices that are higher than your value and answer choices that are lower than your value. If you did the question correctly there will be one answer choice in one group and three answer choices in the other group. Whichever group holds only one answer choice is the correct answer.

So, why does this work? The exam is testing your knowledge about number behavior and identifying trends, but they do not want you to calculate an exact value. They just want you to figure out whether the answer would increase or decrease from that initial value. It is impossible, then, for them to have a correct answer and structure the answer choices any way else. Let's give it a shot!

*For the first problem listed below notice how the initial value for survival % for Species B using Treatment 2 is 40%. There are three answer choices smaller than 40%, but only one larger than 40%. The larger answer choice is correct.

Your Objective: Anticipate the extra step on the problems below.

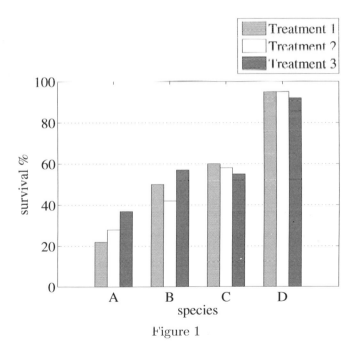

Figure 1

4. Suppose Treatment 2 were repeated, except the bacteria species were shielded from all sources of light. Based on Figure 1, the survival % for species B would most likely be:
   F. less than 20%.
   G. between 20% and 30%.
   H. between 30% and 40%.
   J. greater than 40%.

5. Suppose Treatment 1 were repeated, except the bacteria species were placed in smaller groups. Based on Figure 1, the survival % for species C would most likely be:
   A. less than 60%.
   B. between 60% and 70%.
   C. between 70% and 80%.
   D. greater than 80%.

6. Suppose Treatment 3 were repeated, except the bacteria species were given a more concentrated food medium. Based on Figure 1, the survival % for species D would most likely be:
   F. less than 80%.
   G. between 80% and 85%.
   H. between 85% and 90%.
   J. greater than 90%.

4.3   Outside Knowledge

"
The greatest enemy of knowledge is not ignorance, it is the illusion of knowledge. "   — STEPHEN HAWKING

Outside knowledge questions on the ACT are easy to identify. They typically, nowadays, **appear as the last question** of some of the passages in a section and have science terms or equations as answer choices. It is important to quickly identify an outside knowledge question so time is not wasted going back to the passage attempting to locate the correct answer. If you know the correct answer, great! If you do not, then guess and move on. You NEED NOT be a science master to do well on ACT Science. This represents a small fraction of questions presented on the exam. Feel free to glance over the cheat sheet on the next page, but do not feel the need to memorize it all.

Below are outside knowledge questions that may appear in a passage, but do not need the information in a passage to be answered correctly.

Your Objective: Answer the outside knowledge questions below.

7. When honeybees synthesize proteins, the RNA genetic code is converted into a long polypeptide chain. Which of the following molecules represent the building blocks of this polypeptide chain?
    A. ATP
    B. DNA
    C. Carbohydrates
    D. Amino acids

8. The plants atop the green roof absorb and release various molecules and forms of energy. Which equation best represents the exchange of molecules between the plants and the atmosphere?
    F. light + sugar + water $\rightarrow CO_2 + O_2$
    G. light + water $\rightarrow CO_2 + O_2$ + sugar
    H. light + water + $CO_2 \rightarrow$ sugar + O_2
    J. light + water $\rightarrow CO_2$ + sugar + O_2

9. A protein channel, which facilitates diffusion, helps starch molecules pass through a semi-permeable barrier. Which component of the cell do starch molecules pass through?
    A. Lysosomes
    B. Mitochondria
    C. Cell membrane
    D. Endoplastic Reticulum

10. Monosaccharides are the basic form of carbohydrates and are organic molecules. Which molecule represents a monosaccharide?
    F. NaCl
    G. CO_2
    H. O_3
    J. $C_3H_6O_3$

11. The salt used by the experimenter creates an ionic bond when placed in solution. If a different molecule were chosen for the experiment, the experimenter would choose which molecule to create a similar type of bond?
    A. NaCl
    B. CO_2
    C. O_3
    D. $C_3H_6O_3$

12. At the end of the experiment, the students neutralized the acidic solution in the beaker with an unknown solution. What was the pH of the unknown solution used by the students?
    F. pH 3
    G. pH 5
    H. pH 7
    J. pH 9

13. When calculating the weight of the object, the students multiplied the mass of the object by the gravity of Earth, g. What value of g did the students use?
    A. 1.0 m/s^2
    B. 4.9 m/s^2
    C. 9.8 m/s^2
    D. 12.0 m/s^2

There are, however, certain topics in science that are beneficial to know in preparation for this exam (genetics and energy). Knowing the basic terminology of these topics will help you move through the passages with more confidence.

OUTSIDE KNOWLEDGE CHEAT SHEET

GENETICS

Dominant alleles: Capital letters (T)
Ressessive alleles: Lowercase letters (t)
Heterozygous: Two different alleles (Tt)
Homozygous: Two similar alleles (TT)

*Know how to construct a Punnett square. Assume we are crossing: Bb x bb. The Punnett square would be:

	B	b
b	Bb	bb
b	Bb	bb

Assume we are crossing BbRr x bbrr. Constructing two Punnett squares is best:

	B	b			R	r
b	Bb	bb		r	Rr	rr
b	Bb	bb		r	Rr	rr

ENERGY

Potential energy: Energy at rest. There is typically more potential energy at higher heights and objects at rest.

Kinetic energy: Energy in motion. There is typically more kinetic energy at lower heights and higher speeds.

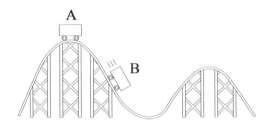

The cart at Point A has more potential energy and less kinetic energy than the cart at Point B.

BIOLOGY	CHEMISTRY	PHYSICS
Gametes: sex cells, which hold half the number of chromosomes	Freezing point of H_2O = 0°C	Total mechanical energy: the sum of potential and kinetic energy of an object
ATP: primary source of energy, produced by mitochondria	Boiling point of H_2O = 100°C	Velocity equation: d = vt
Amino acids: building blocks of protein, contain nitrogen (N)	Solubility: The property of a solute (salt) to dissolve in a solvent (H_2O) to form a solution	Forces: gravity pulls down towards Earth and frictional forces are opposite the direction of motion
Starch: sugars	Radiation: energy leaves an object through a material medium	Circuit units: voltage (volts—V), current (amps—A), resistance (ohms—Ω)
Gene: a combination of related alleles	Convection: energy leaves an object via circulation in fluids	Current and resistance have an inverse relationship
Alleles: the individual pieces of a gene	Conduction: energy leaves an object via direct contant with another object	Positive and negative signs denote direction, not magnitude. For example, -5 m/s is faster than 2 m/s.
Endotherms: warm-blooded	*Understand chemical equations:	Like charges and poles repel, unlike charges and poles attract.
Ectotherms: cold-blooded	$$3H_2 + N_2 \rightarrow 2NH_3$$	
Vertebrates: organisms that have backbones	If 6 moles of hydrogen gas are consumed, how many moles of ammonia are produced? [4]	
Invertebrates: organisms that do not have backbones		

4.4 Chapters 3 and 4 Test: Scientific Method and Last Questions

The chapter test you are about to take will test your knowledge on the skills introduced in the first four chapters. You will be tested on the full slate of questions presented in the ACT Science section. Use this chapter test as the first real test to measure how comfortable you are tackling ACT Science.

A few reminders about what you learned in Chapters 3 and 4:

1. Remember the elements of an experiment: "What are they changing and what are they measuring?"

2. Look for inverse trends on late questions in passages.

3. Anticipate the second step when dealing with last questions. The first step will be there as an incorrect answer choice.

4. Sometimes it is all about outside knowledge. If you know it, great. If not, leave it up to the science Gods.

5. And never forget to, when you get in trouble, stick to our main approach: Finding *Waldo*.

Good luck!

SCIENCE

35 Minutes—40 Questions

DIRECTIONS: There are six passages in this test. Each passage is followed by several questions. After reading a passage, choose the best answer to each question and fill in the corresponding oval on your answer document. You may refer to the passages as often as necessary.

You are NOT permitted to use a calculator on this test.

Passage I

A cross-breeding experiment of common pea plants (*Pisum sativum*) was conducted. This species of pea plant can have the color yellow or green, and its shape can be round or wrinkled. Pea color in *Pisum sativum* is controlled by Gene Y, which has 2 alleles, *Y* and *y*. Pea shape in *Pisum sativum* is controlled by Gene R, which has 2 alleles, *R* and *r*.

Cross 1

Two yellow pea plants, each with genotype *Yy*, were crossed. The color phenotypes and number of offspring are shown in Table 1.

Table 1	
Color phenotype	Number of offspring
yellow	295
green	105

Cross 2

Two round pea plants, each with genotype *Rr*, were crossed. The shape phenotype and number of offspring are shown in Table 2.

Table 2	
Shape phenotype	Number of offspring
round	301
wrinkled	99

Cross 3

Two pea plants, each with genotype *YyRr*, were crossed. The genotype, color phenotype, shape phenotype, and number of offspring are shown in Table 3.

Table 3			
Genotype	Color phenotype	Shape phenotype	Number of offspring
YYRR	yellow	round	25
YYRr	yellow	round	50
YYrr	yellow	wrinkled	11
YyRR	yellow	round	48
YyRr	yellow	round	125
Yyrr	yellow	wrinkled	50
yyRR	green	round	23
yyRr	green	round	52
yyrr	green	wrinkled	16

1. What was the genotype for Gene Y in the offspring from Cross 2?
   A. *YY* only
   B. *Yy* only
   C. Both *YY* and *Yy*
   D. Cannot be determined from the experiment.

2. The percent of offspring from Cross 1 that were green in color was closest to which of the following?
   F. 25 %
   G. 50 %
   H. 75 %
   J. 90 %

3. Based on the results of Cross 1 and 2, which phenotypes are *recessive traits*?
   A. yellow and round
   B. yellow and wrinkled
   C. green and round
   D. green and wrinkled

4. Suppose a scientist wants to produce yellow and wrinkled *Pisum sativum* plants. Based on the results of Cross 3, which of the following crosses would *only* produce offspring with these phenotypes?
   F. *YYrr* and *Yyrr*
   G. *YYRr* and *Yyrr*
   H. *YYRR* and *Yyrr*
   J. *yyrr* and *Yyrr*

5. A graduate student hypothesized that about half of the offspring from Cross 3 would be yellow and round. Are the results of Cross 3 consistent with the student's hypothesis?
   A. Yes; There were 400 total offspring and close to 200 were yellow and round.
   B. Yes; There were 500 total offspring and close to 250 were yellow and round.
   C. No; There were 400 total offspring and close to 250 were yellow and round.
   D. No; There were 500 total offspring and close to 200 were yellow and round.

6. Assume a green and wrinkled *Pisum sativum* plant is crossed with a green and round *Pisum sativum* plant. What percent of offspring will yield the *yyRR* phenotype?
   F. 0 %
   G. 25 %
   H. 50 %
   J. 100 %

Passage II

Graduate students conducted an experiment to investigate the stiffness of cylindrical pipes based on various physical properties.

Throughout each trial, a 10 kg pipe was fixed at both ends with clamps. A load of weight, W, measured in Newtons (N), was placed on the center of each pipe. The pipes were measured for the *extent of deformation*, D, which was recorded in 10^{-3} m (see Figure 1). After the amount of bend was measured, the load was removed. The experiment was repeated for various ambient room temperatures, T.

Figure 1

Young's modulus, E, is a physical parameter of an elastic solid. It measures the force per unit area that is needed to compress a material and is calculated as follows.

$$E = \frac{\text{tensile stress}}{\text{extensional strain}}$$

The graduate students repeated the experiment for various unknown metals (A-D), each with a different value of E.

Study 1

For Trials 1-4, graduate students measured D for a pipe bearing loads of different weights, W (see Table 1). In each trial, $E = 100$ N/m^2 and $T = 25°$C.

Table 1		
Trial	W (N)	D (10^{-3} m)
1	30	2.5
2	40	3.3
3	50	4.2
4	60	5.1

Study 2

For Trials 5-8, graduate students measured D for four different pipes, each having a different E (see Table 2). The pipes were labeled A-D. In each trial, $W = 30$ N and $T = 25°$C.

Table 2			
Trial	Label	E (N/m^2)	D (10^{-3} m)
5	A	50	4.7
6	B	100	2.5
7	C	150	1.3
8	D	200	0.6

Study 3

For Trials 9-12, graduate students measured D for pipes while changing the air temperature of the room (see Table 3). In each trial, $W = 30$ N and $E = 100$ N/m^2.

Table 3		
Trial	T (°C)	D (10^{-3} m)
9	25	2.5
10	26	2.8
11	27	3.1
12	28	3.4

7. According to the results of Study 1, as the load placed on the center of the pipe increased, D:
    A. increased only.
    B. decreased only.
    C. increased, then decreased.
    D. varied, but with no general trend.

8. Suppose, in Study 2, an additional trial were conducted where $E = 175$ N/m^2. The value for D would most likely have been:
    F. 0.6×10^{-3} m
    G. 0.9×10^{-3} m
    H. 1.3×10^{-3} m
    J. 1.7×10^{-3} m

9. In physics textbooks, the amount of work done on a system is calculated as $W \times D$. Which trial yielded the greatest amount of work?
    A. Trial 1
    B. Trial 5
    C. Trial 8
    D. Trial 9

10. The pipe tested in Study 1 was most likely made up of which metal?
    F. Metal A
    G. Metal B
    H. Metal C
    J. Metal D

11. The graduate students wanted to set up conditions that would result in the lowest extent of deformation. Based on the results of Studies 1 and 3, which conditions listed below would the students choose?
    A. A load of 20 N and a laboratory temperature of 20°C
    B. A load of 25 N and a laboratory temperature of 20°C
    C. A load of 25 N and a laboratory temperature of 25°C
    D. A load of 30 N and a laboratory temperature of 25°C

12. Which variable had the same value for all trials tested in Study 2, but did not have the same for all trials tested in Study 1?
    F. The load on the pipe, W (N)
    G. Young's modulus, E (N/m^2)
    H. Laboratory air temperature, T (°C)
    J. Extent of deformation, D (10^{-3}m)

13. According to the information provided, the *force due to gravity* acting on each pipe during the experiment was closest to which of the following?
    A. 10 N
    B. 50 N
    C. 100 N
    D. 150 N

Passage III

Electrical circuits are connections of electrical elements, such as resistors, voltage sources, and current sources. Physics students studied the relationship between voltage, electrical current, and electrical resistance using the circuit shown in Figure 1.

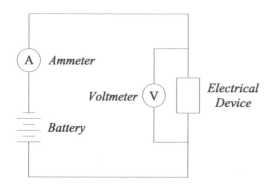

Figure 1

The students measured the electrical current, I, flowing through 3 circuit devices — a filament lamp, an LED, and a diode — as a function of voltage, ε. At each voltage the students also measured the electrical resistance, R, of each circuit device.

Figure 2 shows the data collected comparing I, in milliamperes (mA) and ε, in volts (V) for each device. Figure 3 shows the data collected comparing R, in ohms (Ω) and ε, in volts (V) for each device.

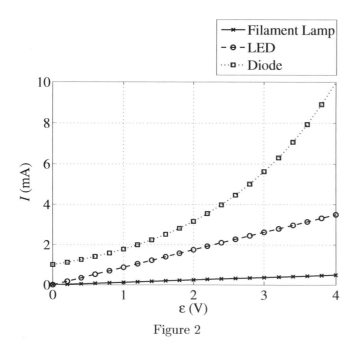

Figure 2

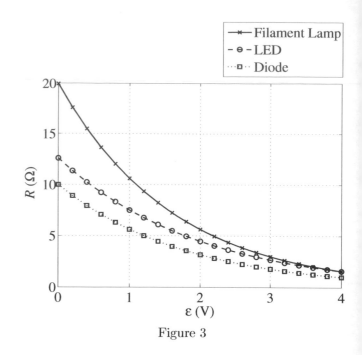

Figure 3

14. According to Figure 3, for each device tested, as the voltage (ε) increased, R:
    F. increased only.
    G. decreased only.
    H. remained constant.
    J. varied, but with no general trend.

15. According to Figure 2, at a voltage of 5 V, the current flowing through the diode would be closest to which of the following?
    A. 1 mA
    B. 8 mA
    C. 10 mA
    D. 14 mA

16. Based on Figures 2 and 3, for each device tested, as the resistance decreased, the current flowing through the device:
    F. increased only.
    G. decreased only.
    H. increased, then decreased.
    J. decreased, then increased.

17. Based on Figures 2 and 3, at a resistance of 5 Ω, the current, I, flowing through the LED is most likely:
    A. less than 1 mA.
    B. between 1 mA and 2 mA.
    C. between 2 mA and 3 mA.
    D. greater than 4 mA.

18. According to Figure 2, which variables were intentionally varied?
    F. The electrical current and the voltage
    G. The electrical current and the type of electrical device
    H. The voltage and the type of electrical device
    J. The voltage and the resistance

19. In physics, if the ratio of voltage, ε, to resistance, R, of an electrical device is constant, the device is said to be "ohmic". A student argued that the LED device should be considered ohmic. Does Figure 3 support the student's statement?
    A. Yes; The diode shows a linear relationship between voltage and resistance.
    B. Yes; The diode shows a nonlinear relationship between voltage and resistance.
    C. No; The diode shows a linear relationship between voltage and resistance.
    D. No; The diode shows a nonlinear relationship between voltage and resistance.

20. According to Figure 3, at a given ε, which electrical device conducted the *least* amount of electrical current?
    F. The filament lamp
    G. The LED
    H. The Diode
    J. All three devices conducted identical amounts of electrical current.

Passage IV

The *serpentinization reaction* occurs in the absence of atmospheric oxygen (O_2) and leads to the formation of *magnetite* (Fe_3O_4):

$$3Fe_2SiO_4 + 2H_2O \rightarrow 2Fe_3O_4 + 3SiO_2 + 3H_2$$

This reaction can be found in places far away from the Earth's atmosphere, typically deep in ocean waters (see Figure 1). *Olivine* (Fe_2SiO_4) is unstable in seawater and reacts to form the mineral magnetite. The production of H_2, which seeps out of the rocks, provides vital energy sources for surrounding microbial species.

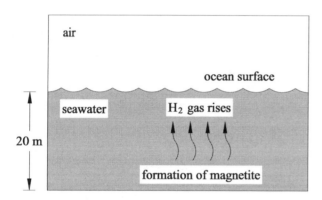

Figure 1

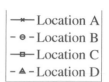

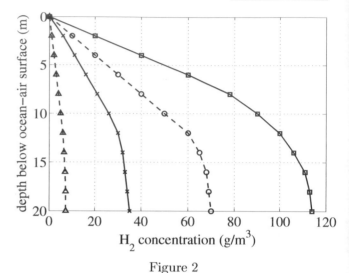

Figure 2

Table 1	
Location	Olivine concentration (kg/m^3)
A	10,201
B	15,038
C	27,402
D	9,293

Scientists conducted a study to measure the different quantities of H_2 gas resulting from serpentinization in 4 different locations within the Pacific Ocean.

Study 1

A device which measures the concentration of hydrogen gas within a 10 m circular radius of water was placed in 4 different locations within the Pacific Ocean. The locations had known quantities of Olivine on the ocean floor. After a period 10 days, the devices were collected and the concentration of hydrogen gas at various depths was recorded (see Figure 2). The various concentrations of Olivine within a 10 m radius of the measuring device are tabulated in Table 1.

Study 2

The scientists repeated the same procedure from Study 1, except a device which measures the concentration of silicon dioxide (SiO_2) was utilized. After collecting the device from the same four locations, they noticed it had been damaged and the data unreadable. The scientists hypothesized that the concentration of silicon dioxide would directly correlate to the concentration of hydrogen gas.

21. Based on the results of Study 1, as the concentration of olivine increases, the concentration of H_2 at depths greater than 0 m:
    A. increases only.
    B. decreases only.
    C. varies, but with no general trend.
    D. remains constant.

22. Based on the description of Study 1, the device covered an area of approximately how many square meters?
    F. 5π m^2
    G. 10π m^2
    H. 50π m^2
    J. 100π m^2

23. Based on Figure 2, the hydrogen gas concentration, in g/m^3, for Location B at a depth of 25 m would be closest to which of the following?
    A. 60 g/m^3
    B. 75 g/m^3
    C. 90 g/m^3
    D. 105 g/m^3

24. According to Figure 2, over the first 20 m below the ocean-air surface, how did the hydrogen gas concentration at Location B compare to the hydrogen gas concentration at Location A? The hydrogen gas concentration at Location B was:
    F. less at each depth.
    G. greater at each depth.
    H. less at some depths but greater at all other depths.
    J. greater at some depths but lesser at all other depths.

25. Consider a 10 m^3 sample of water from Location B at a depth of 20 m below the ocean-air surface. How many grams of hydrogen gas would be present in the sample?
    A. 10 g
    B. 70 g
    C. 100 g
    D. 700 g

26. Suppose a 5 m^3 sample of water from Location D at a depth of 15 m below the ocean air surface were mixed with a 5 m^3 sample of water from Location A at a depth of 15 m. The concentration of hydrogen gas in the resulting solution would be closest to which of the following?
    F. 10 g/m^3
    G. 20 g/m^3
    H. 30 g/m^3
    J. 40 g/m^3

27. Based on the balanced chemical equation in the passage, as 6 moles of olivine are consumed, how many moles of magnetite are produced?
    A. 2
    B. 4
    C. 6
    D. 8

Passage V

The *HgR* gene controls hunger and appetite in blow flies (family *Calliphoridae*). The normal form of this gene (*H*) produces regular hunger habits. A mutated form (*H⁻*) causes abnormal behavior.

Scientists studied the hunger patterns and survival of blow flies that had genotypes *HH*, *HH⁻*, and *H⁻H⁻*. Figure 1 shows the amount of *food searching* (duration of exploration for food) conducted by the blow flies per day. Figure 2 shows the number of food searching events conducted by the blow flies per day. Figure 3 shows how percent survival varied with age for each genotype.

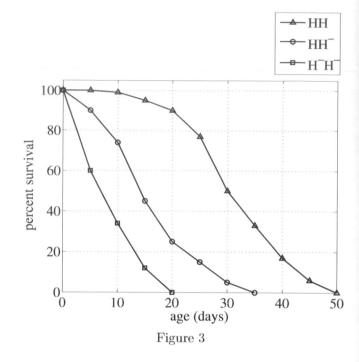

Figure 3

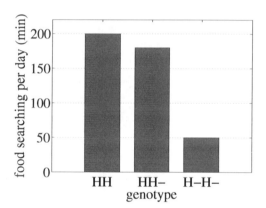

Figure 1

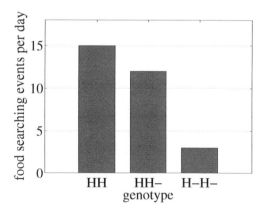

Figure 2

28. Based on Figures 2 and 3, the blow flies that exhibited the most food searching events in a day had a maximum life span of:

F. 20 days
G. 35 days
H. 50 days
J. 65 days

29. According to Figure 1 and other information provided, does a blow fly with two normal alleles for the *HgR* gene spend more or less time exploring for food than a blow fly with two abnormal alleles?

A. More time; According to Figure 1, the blow flies with genotype *HH* spent the most time searching for food.
B. Less time; According to Figure 1, the blow flies with genotype *HH* spent the most time searching for food.
C. More time; According to Figure 1, the blow flies with genotype *H⁻H⁻* spent the most time searching for food.
D. Less time; According to Figure 1, the blow flies with genotype *H⁻H⁻* spent the most time searching for food.

30. According to Figure 2, the food searching events per day for blow flies with the *HH* genotype was approximately how many times as great as that for blow flies with the H^-H^- genotype?

    F. 2

    G. 3

    H. 5

    J. 10

31. A student hypothesized that the blow flies with the mutated alleles of the *HgR* gene would live longer than blow flies with the normal form of the *HgR* gene. Do the results of the study support this hypothesis?

    A. Yes; Blow flies with the *HH* genotype lived the longest.

    B. Yes; Blow flies with the H^-H^- genotype lived the longest.

    C. No; Blow flies with the *HH* genotype lived the longest.

    D. No; Blow flies with the H^-H^- genotype lived the longest.

32. Suppose a blow fly with genotype *HH* is crossed with a blow fly with genotype H^-H^-. Assume 200 offspring are produed. Based on Figure 3, the number of offspring that will survive at the end of 40 days will most likely be closest to which of the following?

    F. 0

    G. 20

    H. 40

    J. 60

33. Suppose a certain population of blow flies all contained the genotype HH^-. If this population were forced to mate with a different population that only contained the genotype H^-H^-, based on Figure 3, the average life span of resulting offspring would be:

    A. less than 35 days.

    B. between 35 and 40 days.

    C. between 40 and 50 days.

    D. greater than 50 days.

Passage VI

Physics students performed the following experiments in their science class:

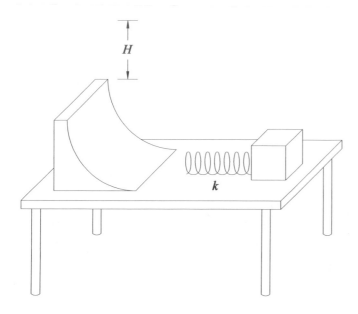

Figure 1

Experiment 1

A quarter-pipe ramp was setup on a long table in the classroom (see Figure 1). A spring, with spring constant $k = 100$ N/m, was fixed at the bottom of the ramp. Three different spheres — Sphere A (1 kg), Sphere B (2 kg), and Sphere C (3 kg) — were dropped from the same initial height, H, of 1 m. The compression of the spring was recorded for multiple trials and the average compression calculated for each sphere. The results of the experiment are shown in Table 1.

Table 1	
Sphere	Average spring compression (m)
A	0.09
B	0.21
C	0.30

Experiment 2

The procedure from Experiment 1 was repeated except the initial height, H, of the spheres was varied. The 9 trials conducted are shown below in Table 2.

Table 2		
Sphere	H (m)	Spring compression (m)
A	2	0.18
A	3	0.27
A	4	0.36
B	2	0.42
B	3	0.63
B	4	0.84
C	2	0.60
C	3	0.90
C	4	1.20

Experiment 3

The procedure from Experiment 1 was repeated except the spring was moved 0.5 m away from the base of the quarter-pipe. The students measured the average spring compression for each sphere. The results of the experiment are shown in Table 3.

Table 3	
Sphere	Average spring compression (m)
A	0.04
B	0.10
C	0.13

34. Based on the passage, which sphere, A or B, had the larger force due to gravity?
    F. Sphere A, because it had the lesser mass.
    G. Sphere A, because it had the greater mass.
    H. Sphere B, because it had the lesser mass.
    J. Sphere B, because it had the greater mass.

35. Suppose 250 N of force was applied to the spring used in Experiment 1. Based on the description of Experiment 1, how many meters would the spring compress?
    A. 2.5 m
    B. 10 m
    C. 100 m
    D. 250 m

36. Based on Experiment 1, as the mass of the spheres increased, the average spring compression:
    F. increased only.
    G. decreased only.
    H. varied, but with no general trend.
    J. remained constant.

37. How did the procedure for measuring the average spring compression in Experiment 3 differ from the procedure for measuring the spring compression in Experiment 2? The procedure for measuring average spring compression in Experiment 3:
    A. required changing the initial height of each sphere, whereas the procedure of Experiment 2 required changing the type of spring.
    B. required changing the initial height of each sphere, whereas the procedure of Experiment 2 required changing the location of the spring.
    C. required changing the location of the spring, whereas the procedure of Experiment 2 required changing the initial height of each sphere.
    D. required changing the location of the spring, whereas the procedure of Experiment 2 required changing the type of spring.

38. One of the students hypothesized that the sphere with the greatest mass would reach the bottom of the ramp with the most *kinetic energy*. Do the results of Experiment 3 support the student's hypothesis?
    F. Yes; Sphere C, which had the greatest mass, produced the greatest average spring compression.
    G. Yes; Sphere A, which had the lowest mass, produced the lowest average spring compression.
    H. No; Sphere C, which had the greatest mass, produced the greatest average spring compression.
    J. No; Sphere A, which had the lowest mass, produced the lowest average spring compression.

39. In Experiment 2, while testing Sphere B, what was the independent variable and what was the dependent variable of the experiment?

	independent	dependent
A.	H	spring compression
B.	H	k
C.	k	spring compression
D.	k	H

40. The *gravitational potential energy*, GPE, of an object is defined as GPE $= mgH$, where m is the mass of the object, g is the acceleration due to gravity (approximately 10 m/s^2), and H is the initial height of the object. Based on the description of Experiment 1, the gravitational potential energy of Sphere C, at the start of the experiment, was:
    F. 10 J
    G. 20 J
    H. 30 J
    J. 40 J

CHAPTER 5

Attacking Conflicting Viewpoints

5.1 Step One

> *Use the same approach you did with figures and tables, now just with text.*

In our experience, the conflicting viewpoints passage is the most polarizing of all the ACT science passages. Students find it to be either the most challenging or the easiest passage of them all. This passage certainly looks different than all of the other passages. However, we assure you that approaching it in the same fashion that you've approached all other passage types will go a long way.

We recommend that some students skip this passage and save it for last. Doing so may be helpful to you depending on how much you like or dislike the passage. And although our mindset regarding locators and *Waldos* still holds true, there are indeed some minor differences. This chapter will walk you through a refined approach to attacking this passage with purpose.

We always recommend jumping straight to the questions...*except when dealing with the conflicting viewpoints passage*, that is. Before you look at the questions, read the **last sentence of the introduction** as well as the **first sentence of each viewpoint**. The last sentence of the introduction gives an overview of what the scientists, students, or hypotheses are about to debate. The first sentence of each viewpoint typically describes the main difference between these viewpoints. Then, having properly oriented yourself with the passage, jump to the questions.

Your Objective: Answer the questions below based on the first sentences of each viewpoint.

CONFLICTING VIEWPOINTS EXAMPLE 1

The sky's blue hue was a popular topic of conversation in the early 17th century. Three 17th century scientists attempt to explain the color of the sky.

Scientist 1

The sky is blue because light from the sun reflects off of ocean waters. At night, when no sunlight is present, the sky is black.

Scientist 2

The sky is blue because shorter wavelengths of light scatter more strongly. The color blue has the shortest wavelength, and therefore scatters prominently throughout the sky.

Scientist 3

I agree with Scientist 2, but with one exception. The color of the sky is actually a mixture of short wavelengths, largely comprised of blue and green.

QUESTIONS

1. Which scientist, if any, would assert that the color of the sky is dependent upon Earth's oceans?
   A. Scientist 1
   B. Scientist 2
   C. Scientist 3
   D. None of the scientists

2. Which scientist, if any, would assert that the color of the sky is dependent upon Earth's clouds?
   F. Scientist 1
   G. Scientist 2
   H. Scientist 3
   J. None of the scientists

3. Which scientist(s), if any, would assert that the color of the sky is dependent upon the different wavelengths of light?
   A. Scientist 2 only
   B. Scientists 1 and 2
   C. Scientists 2 and 3
   D. None of the scientists

5.2   Step Two

Now that you've given yourself a solid foundation with which to tackle the questions of a conflicting viewpoints passage, let's add a layer of strategy to our approach. Step Two is the idea that phrases in the questions have **exact corresponding phrases** in the passages. When you read through a conflicting viewpoints question, do not try to comprehend the problem. Instead, search for important key words or phrases and then find those words or phrases in the passage.

Your Objective: Answer the questions below by finding corresponding phrases in both the questions and the passage.

CONFLICTING VIEWPOINTS EXAMPLE 2

The sky's blue hue was a popular topic of conversation in the early 17th century. Three 17th century scientists attempt to explain the color of the sky.

Scientist 1

The sky is blue because light from the sun reflects off of ocean waters. Water, which has a high reflective coefficient, is able to reflect most of the light it receives back into the atmosphere. The majority of the Earth is covered in water, creating the sky's rich blue hue during the day. However, since some of the light enters the water due to refraction, not all light is reflected. At night, when no sunlight is present, the sky is black.

Scientist 2

The sky is blue because the shorter wavelengths of light are scattered more strongly. The color blue has the shortest wavelength, and therefore scatters prominently throughout the sky. The human eye then sees the color blue when looking towards the sky.

Scientist 3

I agree with Scientist 2, but with two exceptions. Blue does not have the shortest wavelength. The color of the sky is actually a mixture of short wavelengths, largely comprised of blue and green. Blue, however, is slightly more dominant than green due to its shorter wavelength. Furthermore, the human eye will not see the color blue when looking closely at the sun. The light coming directly from the sun travels a straight path to the human eye, ridding the light of scattered particles. The human eye, in this case, is only able to see longer wavelengths of light, which translate to colors like red and orange.

QUESTIONS

4. The present day *electromagnetic spectrum* shows the color purple to have the shortest wavelength. This evidence *weakens*, if at all, the viewpoint of which scientist?
   F. Scientist 1
   G. Scientist 2
   H. Scientist 3
   J. None of the scientists

5. Suppose ocean waters contained a layer of particles on its surface that yielded a low reflective coefficient. This discovery would *weaken* the viewpoint(s) of which scientist?
   A. Scientist 1 only
   B. Scientist 2 only
   C. Scientists 1 and 2
   D. Scientists 3 and 4

6. Assume that light from the sun is comprised of all wavelengths of light except blue. The present day *electromagnetic spectrum* shows the color purple to have the shortest wavelength and the color red to have the longest wavelength. Based on this information, Scientist 3 would most likely agree that the human eye would perceive the sky as:
   F. purple, because light from the sun reflects off of ocean waters.
   G. red, because light from the sun reflects off of ocean waters.
   H. purple, because shorter wavelengths of light are scattered more strongly.
   J. red, because longer wavelengths of light are scattered more strongly.

5.3   The Irrelevant Argument

Suppose a question on a conflicting viewpoints passage refers to Viewpoint A. The ACT will often display the main argument of other viewpoints in the question or answer choices. If you see these arguments as answer choices, feel free to eliminate them since they do not pertain to the viewpoint referred to in the question. Or, suppose you see the main argument of Viewpoint B in the question, and the question is referring you to Viewpoint A. In that case, the correct answer is typically something along the lines of, "Has no effect on Viewpoint A".

Again, think of the conflicting viewpoints passage as a debate. If you and your friends are debating about the next best baseball player and another person enters the conversation talking about basketball, their viewpoint has no bearing on your debate. The same goes for questions like these on the ACT.

Your Objective: Answer the irrelevant argument questions below.

CONFLICTING VIEWPOINTS EXAMPLE 3

The sky's blue hue was a popular topic of conversation in the early 17th century. Three 17th century scientists attempt to explain the color of the sky.

Scientist 1

The sky is blue because light from the sun reflects off of ocean waters. Water, which has a high reflective coefficient, is able to reflect most of the light it receives back into the atmosphere. The majority of the Earth is covered in water, creating the sky's rich blue hue during the day. However, since some of the light enters the water due to refraction, not all light is reflected. At night, when no sunlight is present, the sky is black.

Scientist 2

The sky is blue because the shorter wavelengths of light are scattered more strongly. The color blue has the shortest wavelength, and therefore scatters prominently throughout the sky. The human eye then sees the color blue when looking towards the sky.

Scientist 3

I agree with Scientist 2, but with two exceptions. Blue does not have the shortest wavelength. The color of the sky is actually a mixture of short wavelengths, largely comprised of blue and green. Blue, however, is slightly more dominant than green due to its shorter wavelength. Furthermore, the human eye will not see the color blue when looking closely at the sun. The light coming directly from the sun travels a straight path to the human eye, ridding the light of scattered particles. The human eye, in this case, is only able to see longer wavelengths of light, which translate to colors like red and orange.

QUESTIONS

7. Suppose ocean waters dried up and were eliminated from the surface of Earth. What impact, if any, would this have on Scientist 3's explanation?
    A. It would prove that the explanation is correct.
    B. It would have no impact on the explanation.
    C. It would weaken the explanation.
    D. It would support the explanation, but not prove that the explanation is correct.

8. The present day *electromagnetic spectrum* shows the color purple to have the shortest wavelength. How does this information impact, if at all, Scientist 1's viewpoint?
    F. It would prove that the explanation is correct.
    G. It would have no impact on the explanation.
    H. It would weaken the explanation.
    J. It would support the explanation, but not prove that the explanation is correct.

9. A student hypothesized that air particles tend to attract packets of light that have shorter wavelengths. How does this information impact, if at all, Scientist 1's viewpoint?
    A. It would prove that the explanation is correct.
    B. It would have no impact on the explanation.
    C. It would weaken the explanation.
    D. It would support the explanation, but not prove that the explanation is correct.

5.4 Chapter Test: Conflicting Viewpoints

The Conflicting Viewpoints test is a bit different than previous chapter tests. The following 6 passages are all conflicting viewpoints passages. You need not time yourself on this chapter test. Instead, use this test as an opportunity to practice your conflicting viewpoints approach.

Remember your steps:

1. Read the last sentence of the introduction, then the first sentence of each viewpoint. The goal is to find the main differences between the viewpoints.

2. Find phrases in the passages that exactly match those in the questions. Your mission is to locate, not to comprehend.

If you stick to the proper mindset and try to interpret the text just as you did figures and tables in other passages, your progress will be reflected in this chapter test. If you find yourself using your comprehensive skills to determine correct answers, remember: Doing so may help you in the short run but will certainly limit your potential to improve your ACT Science score.

Good luck!

Passage I

A teacher in a chemistry class placed two beakers with pure water inside of a fume hood. The teacher added a small quantity of salt to one of the beakers and stirred the solution until the salt solute was completely dissolved. Then, the teacher added an unknown solid metal to the solutions. The metal reacted heavily with the salty water, causing a spark, but did not react with the pure water.

The teacher asked three students to explain what had occurred.

Student 1

The metal has a rough surface that produced friction with the salts in the water. Once the metal touched the salt particles, heat was generated from the frictional force between the metallic surface and the salts. It was this heat which caused the spark in the water. The salts, therefore, must have also contained a rough surface to produce the proper amount of friction. Without any salts present in the pure water, there were no particles available to produce friction with the metallic surface.

Student 2

The metal has a charged ionic surface that interacted with the salts in the water. Once the surface of the metal touched the salty water the positive and negative charged particles reacted with one another, causing the spark. The metal, therefore, must have contained a charged center to hold the ions on its surface. Without any charged particles present in the pure water, it is evident that no reaction would have occurred.

Student 3

I agree with Student 2, but with one exception. The metal did not contain a charged center. The ionic surface is held together through ionic bonds between the charged particles. This forms an outer layer on the surface of the metal, which reacted with the salt particles in the water. Had the metal contained a charged center, it would have reacted with its own outer layer and grounded any positive or negative charges on its surface.

1. The salt solute the teacher added to one of the beakers could have been which of the following compounds?
    A. H_2
    B. CO_2
    C. NaCl
    D. O_2

2. Which of the student(s) would agree that the metal was charged before being placed in the beakers?
    F. Student 1 only
    G. Students 2 only
    H. Students 1 and 2
    J. Students 2 and 3

3. Student 1's explanation relates *best* to which experiment?
    A. A kite flying during a thunderstorm.
    B. A ball thrown up in the air.
    C. A block sliding across sandpaper.
    D. An acid solution neutralized with a base solution.

4. Do Students 2 and 3 differ in their explanation as to why a spark occurred?
    F. No; both students claim the charged outer surface of the metal caused a spark.
    G. No; both students claim the charged center of the metal caused a spark.
    H. Yes; Student 2 argues the charged surface caused a spark, whereas Student 3 argues the charged center caused the spark.
    J. Yes; Student 2 argues the charged center caused a spark, whereas Student 3 argues the charged surface caused the spark.

5. Suppose the experiment is repeated with another metal having a smooth uncharged surface, but a charged center. Which of the students, if any, would claim that this metal would cause a spark with the salty water?
    A. Student 1
    B. Student 2
    C. Student 3
    D. None of the students

6. Lightning is produced when negative and positive charged particles in the clouds come in close proximity of one another, creating a spark. Which viewpoint(s) best help to describe the natural phenomenon known as lightning?

F. Student 1 only
G. Student 3 only
H. Students 2 and 3
J. All of the students

7. Suppose the teacher conducted the same experiment, but used an *acetone* (C_3H_6O) solvent instead of water in the beakers. Based on the teacher's demonstration and the 3 viewpoints, how would this affect the results of the experiment?

A. No reaction would occur in the salty solution.
B. A spark would occur in the pure acetone solution.
C. The salt would dissolve readily in the acetone.
D. Cannot be determined from the given information.

Passage II

Four early 1900s scientists discuss atomic structure, specifically the architecture of the atom. They attempt to explain the locations of electrons, protons, and neutrons within an atom.

Scientist 1

Atoms consist of positively charged centers called *nuclei.* Since the nuclei are positively charged, they must contain protons. The nucleus of the atom is the most dense, holding the most mass in a tiny space, whereas the area outside the nucleus is not very dense. Because foreign particles do not experience deflection when within close proximity of an atom, electrons must be located outside of the nucleus. The location of the neutron is impossible to pinpoint because of its neutral charge.

Scientist 2

I agree with Scientist 1, but with one exception. The neutron must be located within the nucleus. The mass-to-volume ratio of the nucleus is too large for the nucleus to only contain protons. There must be an additional subatomic particle located within the center and, due to the positive nature of the nucleus, that particle cannot be the electron.

Scientist 3

Atoms consist of positively charged centers called *nucleoid regions.* The region is not very dense, but does house most of the positively charged subatomic particles. Some protons exist outside of this region, however. Because foreign particles experience high amounts of deflection when within close proximity of an atom, neutrons and electrons must be located outside of the nucleus. The electron is too small to cause the high frequency of deflections alone.

Scientist 4

I agree with Scientist 3, but with one exception. An identical amount of protons exist outside of the nucleoid region, as well as inside. The mass-to-volume ratio of the nucleus is too small to house the majority of protons. Taking into account the high frequency of deflections outside of the nucleoid region, it is more probable for an increased number of protons to be located outside of this region.

8. Which of the scientists, if any, claimed that the atom has a positively charged center?
   F. Scientists 1 and 2
   G. Scientists 3 and 4
   H. All of the scientists
   J. None of the scientists

9. The positively charged center of which scientist's model is most massive?
   A. Scientist 1
   B. Scientist 2
   C. Scientist 3
   D. Scientist 4

10. According to Scientist 1, as one moves farther away from the center of the nucleus, the density of the atom:
   F. increases.
   G. decreases.
   H. remains constant.
   J. varies, but with no general trend.

11. It was eventually proven that *all* protons within an atom are located inside the nucleus. This discovery is most *inconsistent* with which scientist?
   A. Scientist 1
   B. Scientist 2
   C. Scientist 3
   D. Scientist 4

12. Suppose a neutral metallic ball is brought into contact with a positively charged rod. Because charges of like sign repel one another, more positive particles aggregate to the center of the ball than the outer layer. Would Scientist 3 agree or disagree with the distribution of positive particles within the ball, assuming the ball mimics the same mechanics as an atom?
   F. Agree, because the center region of the atom has more positive particles than the outer region.
   G. Agree, because the center region of the atom has fewer positive particles than the outer region.
   H. Disagree, because the center region of the atom has more positive particles than the outer region.
   J. Disagree, because the center region of the atom has fewer positive particles than the outer region.

13. Scientist 1, when attempting to pinpoint the location of the neutron, was most likely using which device?
    A. A balance, which measures mass.
    B. An electrometer, which measures electrical charge.
    C. A barometer, which measures pressure.
    D. A lux meter, which measures the intensity of light.

14. Science textbooks show the evolution of atomic structure from its inception to present day. Which scientist best models the present day atomic structure?
    F. Scientist 1
    G. Scientist 2
    H. Scientist 3
    J. Scientist 4

Passage III

The Arctic tern (*Sterna paradisaea*) has one of the longest migration patterns of any bird. Seeing two summers every year, the Arctic tern begins its journey from the Arctic breeding grounds and heads towards the Antarctic coast. In order to have enough energy for the migration, the Arctic tern has refined methods for acquiring and storing energy.

Consider the 3 hypotheses explaining how the Arctic tern acquires the necessary energy for migration and how that energy is stored during flight.

Hypothesis 1

The Arctic tern acquires energy through consumption of fish during the flight. The bird flies down to the surface of the water and catches fish that are nearby. Without pausing during flight, the Arctic tern is able to consume the prey and continue with migration. The energy is stored mostly in muscle cells due to the high protein content of fish. When energy is necessary to continue migration, the Arctic tern prioritizes the break down of muscle cells.

Hypothesis 2

The Arctic tern acquires energy through consumption of invertebrates. The bird lands and preys on invertebrates that are nearby. Flight must be paused briefly during the consumption of invertebrates, after which the Arctic tern immediately restarts its flight. The energy from the prey is stored mostly in fat cells due to the high energy content of lipids. When energy is necessary to continue migration, the Arctic tern prioritizes the break down of fat cells.

Hypothesis 3

The Arctic tern acquires energy through consumption of berries. The bird will stop flight and build a nest for a duration of 1-2 days. Here, the Arctic tern gathers enough berries necessary in order to ensure an adequate amount of energy to continue migration. No berries are consumed during flight. The energy acquired from berries is mostly stored in fat cells due to the high energy content of lipids. When energy is necessary to continue migration, the Arctic tern prioritizes the break down of fat cells.

15. Which hypothesis, if any, asserts that the Arctic tern acquires energy through the consumption of organisms from the *Plantae* kingdom?
    A. Hypothesis 1
    B. Hypothesis 2
    C. Hypothesis 3
    D. None of the hypotheses

16. Which hypothesis, if any, asserts that the Arctic tern never stops its flight during migration?
    F. Hypothesis 1
    G. Hypothesis 2
    H. Hypothesis 3
    J. None of the hypotheses

17. Which of the following statements disagrees with all 3 hypotheses?
    A. The Arctic tern never stops flying during migration.
    B. The Arctic tern will delay flying during migration.
    C. Energy acquired by the Arctic tern through consumption is never used during flight.
    D. Energy acquired by the Arctic tern through consumption is used during flight.

18. A different species of bird is observed during migration. It is noted that the wings of this bird operate most efficiently when extracting energy from proteins. Does this observation help support Hypothesis 1?
    F. Yes, because the hypothesis states that the Arctic tern prioritizes the break down of muscle cells.
    G. Yes, because the hypothesis states that the Arctic tern prioritizes the break down of fat cells.
    H. No, because the hypothesis states that the Arctic tern prioritizes the break down of muscle cells.
    J. No, because the hypothesis states that the Arctic tern prioritizes the break down of fat cells.

19. A scientist studying an ecosystem notices a dangerously high level of honey bee ants (a native invertebrate) in the region. The scientist decides to introduce the Arctic tern into the region in hopes of eliminating some of the honey bee ant population. Which hypotheses would best support the decision made by the scientist?
    A. Hypothesis 1 only
    B. Hypothesis 2 only
    C. Hypotheses 1 and 2
    D. Hypotheses 1 and 3

20. Suppose it is discovered that a majority of bird species prefer to migrate to locations near the equator than the Arctic or Antarctic regions. How does this discovery strengthen or weaken the 3 hypotheses?
    F. This discovery strengthens Hypothesis 1.
    G. This discovery weakens Hypotheses 2 and 3.
    H. This discovery strengthens Hypotheses 2 and 3.
    J. This discovery has no effect on the hypotheses.

21. When the Arctic tern breaks down cells to extract energy for flight, which high-energy molecule is most likely produced?
    A. Amino acids
    B. Glucose
    C. ATP
    D. Lipids

Passage IV

Introduction

Blood coagulation, or clotting, is the transformation of blood from a liquid into a solid gel. Formation of a clot strengthens the seal over a break in a blood vessel. As blood in the proximity of the vessel solidifies, it can no longer flow.

The *clotting cascade* (see Figure 1) helps visualize the process. When a cut occurs, *platelets* attach to *collagen fibers* and become sticky. This seal is reinforced by *fibrin*, which is a derivative of *fibrinogen*. Fibrin is formed when *prothrombin* is activated, forming *thrombin*. Thrombin catalyzes the conversion of fibrinogen into fibrin. The threads of fibrin form the final step of the blood clot.

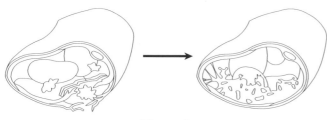

Figure 1

Hemophilia, a genetic mutation, causes excessive bleeding from even minor cuts and bruises. Four hypotheses discuss how hemophilia could interfere with the blood clotting process.

Hypothesis 1

Hemophilia changes the genetic code of prothrombin produced by the body. The outer protein coat is altered, which disables the enzyme that converts prothrombin into thrombin from properly identifying the molecule. Because thrombin is never produced fibrinogen is never converted into fibrin. Thus, the final step of the blood clot never occurs.

Hypothesis 2

Hemophilia changes the genetic code of fibrin produced by the body. The outer protein coat is altered to such a point that the body believes it to be foreign. White blood cells then attack fibrin when produced, never allowing the final step of blood clotting to occur.

Hypothesis 3

Hemophilia changes the genetic code of fibrin produced by the body. The mechanism for fibrin to merge together and form the blood clot is disabled. Even though the other molecules of the blood clotting process are unaltered, the disabling of fibrin prevents the final step of blood clotting from occurring.

Hypothesis 4

Hemophilia changes the genetic code of prothrombin produced by the body. When active, prothrombin produces excess fibrinogen instead of thrombin. Because thrombin is never produced fibrinogen is never converted into fibrin. Thus, the final step of the blood clot never occurs.

22. Both Hypothesis 2 and 3 indicate that the genetic code of which molecule is altered by the genetic disorder hemophilia?
    F. Prothrombin
    G. Thrombin
    H. Fibrinogen
    J. Fibrin

23. According to the information provided, is prothrombin *directly* involved in the formation of a blood clot?
    A. Yes, because the threads of prothrombin form the final step of the blood clot.
    B. Yes, because the threads of fibrin form the final step of the blood clot.
    C. No, because the threads of prothrombin form the final step of the blood clot.
    D. No, because the threads of fibrin form the final step of the blood clot.

24. In which of the following ways do Hypotheses 1 and 2 differ with regard to how hemophilia affects the blood clotting process? Hypothesis 1 asserts that hemophilia changes the genetic code of:
    F. prothrombin, which prevents conversion into thrombin; Hypothesis 2 asserts that fibrin is altered.
    G. prothrombin, which prevents conversion into fibrin; Hypothesis 2 asserts that fibrin is altered.
    H. fibrin, which prevents conversion into thrombin; Hypothesis 2 asserts that prothrombin is altered.
    J. fibrin, which prevents conversion into prothrombin; Hypothesis 2 asserts that prothrombin is altered.

25. A substance, which behaves identically to thrombin, is injected into a patient with hemophilia. Would Hypothesis 3 or Hypothesis 4 argue that this patient would experience normal blood clotting?
    A. Hypothesis 3, which argues hemophilia stops the production of healthy thrombin.
    B. Hypothesis 3, which argues hemophilia stops the production of healthy fibrin.
    C. Hypothesis 4, which argues hemophilia stops the production of healthy thrombin.
    D. Hypothesis 4, which argues hemophilia stops the production of healthy fibrin.

26. Suppose it were discovered that a secondary effect of hemophilia is an abnormally low concentration of thrombin in the blood. This discovery would best agree with which hypotheses?
    F. Hypotheses 1 and 3
    G. Hypotheses 1 and 4
    H. Hypotheses 2 and 3
    J. Hypotheses 1, 3, and 4

27. Suppose healthy fibrin molecules were injected into a patient with hemophilia. Which hypotheses, if any, would support the claim that this patient would experience normal blood clotting?
    A. Hypotheses 1 and 4
    B. Hypotheses 2 and 3
    C. All four hypotheses
    D. None of the hypotheses

28. Assume that hemophilia does not cause any abnormal disturbances in the body's *immune system*. This statement is *inconsistent* with which hypothesis?
    F. Hypothesis 1
    G. Hypothesis 2
    H. Hypothesis 3
    J. Hypothesis 4

Passage V

A teacher performed a solubility test in front of a chemistry class. 10 mg of an unknown solute was placed into a reaction tube at 25°C with 0.25 mL of water, a *polar solvent*. The mixture was stirred with a fire-polished stirring rod. After waiting for two minutes the class was asked to record whether or not the solute dissolved in the solvent. The experiment was repeated using toluene, a *nonpolar solvent*, instead of water.

The teacher listed some properties of each solvent (see Table 1).

Table 1	
Solvent Tested	Properties
Water	Contains an -OH group and ionic
Toluene	An aromatic hydrocarbon

The teacher then asked 3 students to recite their observations and state whether or not the solute was polar or nonpolar.

Student 1

The solute dissolved in the water solvent, but did not dissolve in the toluene solvent. Polar molecules seem to be attracted to each other because of the differences in charge. Without this difference, the molecules would not exhibit any force of attraction. Because of the difference in charge and the force of attraction created, the solute used in the experiment must have also been polar. When the solute was placed in toluene there was no force of attraction created since toluene is a nonpolar solvent.

Student 2

I agree with Student 1 but with one exception. Not all polar molecules are attracted to each other. The solute used in the experiment dissolved in the water because it had a dipole moment (a measure of polarity) that matched that of the water molecules. Had the solute been more polar, or less polar, it would not have dissolved as readily in the water. This also holds true for the toluene solvent. A nonpolar solvent like toluene has a lower polarity difference than the solute in question. Due to the discrepancy in polar differences, a solution was not possible.

Student 3

The solute dissolved in both the water solvent and toluene solvent. Because the solute was able to dissolve in both solvents, it must have been nonpolar. Nonpolar molecules have no charge and would not disrupt the charge of the water molecules. Thus, the water can dissolve the nonpolar solute into solution. This also holds true for the toluene solvent since there would be no charges in either the solute or solvent. Nonpolar solvents seem to be the most useful for dissolving almost any solute.

29. Which is the most likely reason why the teacher waited two minutes before allowing students to record their observations?
    A. To allow the unknown solute to dissolve into solution
    B. To allow the temperature of the solution to reach room temperature
    C. To allow the solution to settle after stirring
    D. To allow the temperature of the solute to equal the temperature of the solvent

30. Which student, if any, asserts that the solute used in the experiment was nonpolar?
    F. Student 1
    G. Student 2
    H. Student 3
    J. None of the students

31. The teacher declared to the class that the solute used in the experiment was polar. This statement agrees with which of the following student(s)?
    A. Student 1 only
    B. Student 3 only
    C. Students 1 and 2
    D. Students 2 and 3

32. Which of the following statements most *weakens* the viewpoint of Student 3?
    F. Polar solvents dissolve polar solutes.
    G. Polar solvents do not dissolve polar solutes.
    H. Nonpolar solvents dissolve polar solutes.
    J. Nonpolar solvents do not dissolve polar solutes.

33. Suppose an additional trial utilizing a nonpolar solute was conducted. Based on Student 1's explanation, would the solute dissolve in the water or toluene solvent?
    A. Water, because Student 1 states that polar solvents dissolve polar solutes.
    B. Water, because Student 1 states that polar solvents dissolve nonpolar solutes.
    C. Toluene, because Student 1 states that polar solvents dissolve polar solutes.
    D. Toluene, because Student 1 states that polar solvents dissolve nonpolar solutes.

34. *Ligroin*, a commonly used laboratory solvent, is a mixture of aliphatic hydrocarbons. Based on Table 1 and other information provided, Student 3 would argue that Ligroin could dissolve which chemical compound(s)?
    F. NaCl
    G. CH_4
    H. Both NaCl and CH_4
    J. Neither NaCl nor CH_4

Passage VI

Three graduate students conducted a study to analyze the effects of gravity on snowboarders riding a U-shaped half-pipe (see Figure 1).

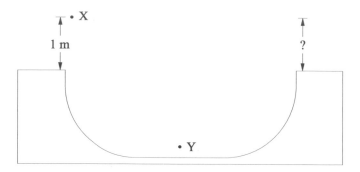

Figure 1

Procedure

Two different snowboarders were chosen for the study. A 50 kg athlete, Snowboarder A, and a 60 kg athlete, Snowboarder B, were released from rest, at different times, from Point X on the left side of U-shaped half-pipe (neglect the effects of friction). The snowboarders were told to launch as far up the right side of the half-pipe without exerting extra force. The maximum height attained in the air on the right side of the half-pipe for each snowboarder was recorded. In addition, the gravitational potential energy (GPE) and kinetic energy (KE) of both snowboarders at points X and Y were calculated (see Table 1).

	Table 1			
Athlete	Maximum height (m)	GPE at X (J)	KE at X (J)	KE at Y (J)
A	1	500	0	500
B	1	600	n/a	600

The 3 graduate students discussed the results of the study.

Graduate Student 1

The two athletes reached the same maximum height on the half-pipe because the acceleration due to Earth's gravity was constant. Without a constant gravitational force, the maximum height reached would vary. In addition, the starting positions of the athletes must be identical to achieve the same height on the other side of the half-pipe, which was the case in this study. The difference in mass between the athletes had no effect on the results.

Graduate Student 2

The two athletes reached the same maximum height on the half-pipe because the difference in their masses was negligible. Had we conducted the study using a bigger difference in starting mass, there would have been a noticeable change in the maximum height attained on the right side of the half-pipe. The gravitational attraction between Earth and the athletes had no effect on the results of this study.

Graduate Student 3

The two athletes reached the same maximum height on the half-pipe because their initial positions were identical. The gravitational attraction between Earth and the athletes had no effect on the results of this study. Furthermore, the difference in mass between the athletes played no role whatsoever in the mechanics of the study.

35. Which graduate student(s) would agree that gravity played a significant role in the results of the study?
    A. Graduate Student 1 only
    B. Graduate Student 3 only
    C. Graduate Students 1 and 2
    D. Graduate Students 2 and 3

36. During the experiment, the device used to calculate energy was disrupted the for KE at Point X of Athlete B. According to Table 1 and Figure 1, the value for KE at Point X for Athlete B is:
    F. 0 J
    G. 50 J
    H. 500 J
    J. 600 J

37. Suppose a 2 kg sphere underwent the same procedure in the study conducted by the graduate students. Which graduate student(s), if any, would assert that the sphere would reach a maximum height of 1 m?
    A. Graduate Student 1 only
    B. Graduate Students 1 and 3
    C. Graduate Students 2 and 3
    D. None of the Graduate Students

38. Consider the theoretical experiment where a 7.0 kg bowling ball and a 0.6 kg tennis ball are dropped from the same height. The fall time of each ball is found to be identical. Would this finding mostly *weaken* the viewpoint of Graduate Student 1 or Graduate Student 2?
    F. Graduate Student 1; According to the student, a difference in mass would NOT have an effect on the results.
    G. Graduate Student 1; According to the student, a difference in mass would have an effect on the results.
    H. Graduate Student 2; According to the student, a difference in mass would NOT have an effect on the results.
    J. Graduate Student 2; According to the student, a difference in mass would have an effect on the results.

39. Suppose the procedure were repeated except the initial position (Point X) of both athletes was 2 m above the half-pipe. Based on the passage, what would most likely have been the maximum height attained on the right side of the half-pipe by the athletes?
    A. 1 m
    B. 2 m
    C. 10 m
    D. 20 m

40. The gravity of Earth, g, has an approximate value of 9.81 m/s^2. The gravity of Earth's Moon has an approximate value of 1.63 m/s^2. Suppose the procedure were repeated on the surface of Earth's Moon instead of on the surface of Earth. According to Graduate Student 3, how would this affect the results of the study?
    F. The maximum height reached by both athletes would be lower.
    G. The GPE at Point X would not equal the KE at Point Y.
    H. The loss of friction on Earth's Moon would prevent the completion of the experiment.
    J. It would have no effect on the results of the study.

CHAPTER 6

PUTTING IT ALL TOGETHER: PRACTICE TEST 1

" *Success is a journey, not a destination.* " — ARTHUR ASHE

If you have made it through all 5 chapters and arrived at this page, we salute you. We hope what you have learned has helped you become more comfortable tackling ACT Science.

The bittersweet aspect of tutoring is that one day, if your students are well prepared and have success, you as the tutor have nothing more to share. Well, we have reached that point in our preparation. Take what you have learned from this guide and attack the practice tests to follow with confidence.

It has been my pleasure to teach you what I have learned through my experience as a test prep tutor. As a reminder, if you ever have any questions regarding ACT Science, please do not hesitate to reach out to me: michael@privateprep.com. For science!

Good luck!

SCIENCE

35 Minutes—40 Questions

DIRECTIONS: There are six passages in this test. Each passage is followed by several questions. After reading a passage, choose the best answer to each question and fill in the corresponding oval on your answer document. You may refer to the passages as often as necessary.

You are NOT permitted to use a calculator on this test.

Passage I

Scientists collected data on native tiger species within the Asia-Pacific region. If enough data could be gathered for a particular species, then the species was placed within one of five categories on the *Red List* (a system assessing the global conservation status of a species). The data collected is shown below in Table 1.

Table 1	
Category	Percent of species
Least concern (LC)	10
Vulnerable (VU)	20
Endangered (EN)	5
Critically endangered (CR)	30
Extinct (EX)	25

The scientists attempted to determine the cause of the depreciation of tiger populations in the Asia-Pacific region. The Asian black bear (*U. thibetanus*) is one of the main predators of tigers. The scientists collected yearly data from 2002-2010 on the *U. thibetanus* population versus tiger populations in the Asia-Pacific region. They attempted to identify whether the populations matched a predator-prey model (see Figure 1).

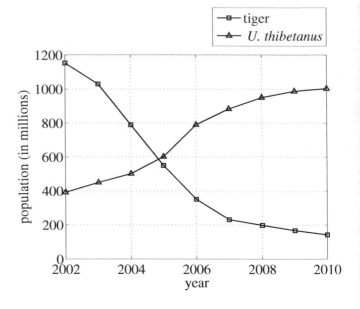

Figure 1

1. According to Figure 1, in what year were the tiger and the Asian black bear populations nearly identical?
   A. 2003
   B. 2005
   C. 2007
   D. 2009

2. Of the tiger species placed in a category on the Red List, based on Table 1, what percent are NOT extinct?
    F. 25%
    G. 45%
    H. 65%
    J. 75%

3. Assume that all Asian black bears were removed from the Asia-Pacific region in 2010. Based on Figure 1 and other information provided, the tiger population in the region in the year 2014 would most likely have been:
    A. less than or equal to 10 million.
    B. between 10 million and 100 million.
    C. between 100 million and 200 million.
    D. greater than 200 million.

4. Based on Table 1, what percent of tiger species did the scientists *fail* to place in one of the Red List categories?
    F. 10%
    G. 20%
    H. 30%
    J. 40%

5. Generally, predator-prey models suggest that the population of a predator and its prey have an inverse relationship. Based on Figure 1, do the tiger and *U. thibetanus* populations in the Asia-Pacific region fit a predator-prey model?
    A. No; In the Asia-Pacific region, as the tiger population decreases, the *U. thibetanus* population increases.
    B. No; In the Asia-Pacific region, as the tiger population decreases, the *U. thibetanus* population decreases.
    C. Yes; In the Asia-Pacific region, as the tiger population decreases, the *U. thibetanus* population increases.
    D. Yes; In the Asia-Pacific region, as the tiger population decreases, the *U. thibetanus* population decreases.

6. Suppose 300 tiger species were sorted into Red List categories and the percentages calculated in Table 1. Approximately how many tiger species would be considered Vulnerable (VU) or Endangered (EN)?
    F. 25
    G. 75
    H. 150
    J. 300

Passage II

In chemistry the *mean free path*, λ, is the average distance traveled by an atom between consecutive collisions with other atoms. This distance is dependent on various parameters, such as atomic radius, temperature, and pressure. Table 1 lists the name, symbol, and atomic radii of 4 metals. Figure 1 shows, for each metal, the mean free path (in nm) as a function of temperature (in °C) at a pressure of 760 mm Hg. Figure 2 shows, for each metal, the mean free path (in nm) as a function of pressure (mm Hg) at a temperature of 270 K.

Element name	Symbol	Atomic radii (pm)
Lithium	Li	145
Sodium	Na	180
Potassium	K	220
Rubidium	Rb	235

Table 1

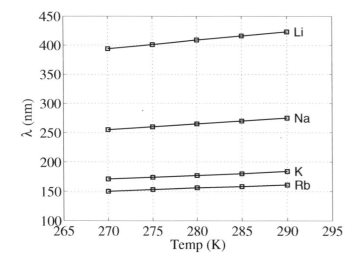

Figure 1

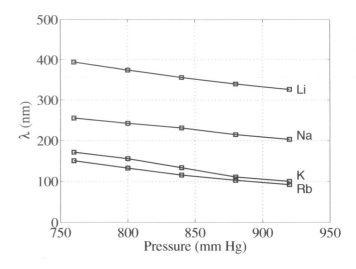

Figure 2

7. According to Figure 2, for a given element, as the pressure increases the mean free path:
    A. increases only.
    B. decreases only.
    C. increases, then decreases.
    D. remains constant.

8. According to Figure 1, at 285 K and 760 mm Hg, what is the order of metals from longest λ to shortest λ?
    F. Li, Na, K, Rb
    G. Na, Li, K, Rb
    H. Rb, K, Na, Li
    J. Li, Rb, K, Na

9. Based on Figure 2, for the Li and Na samples at 270 K, compared to λ for Li, approximately how much shorter is λ for Na?
    A. 100 nm
    B. 125 nm
    C. 150 nm
    D. 175 nm

10. Based on Table 1 and Figure 1, as atomic radii increases, the mean free path:

   F. increases only.

   G. decreases only.

   H. increases, then decreases.

   J. decreases, then increases.

11. Cesium (Cs) is an alkali metal located in Group 1 on the periodic table with an atomic radius of 260 pm. Based on Table 1 and Figure 1, at 760 mm Hg and 270 K, λ for Cs would be approximately:

   A. 120 pm

   B. 160 pm

   C. 200 pm

   D. 240 pm

12. In chemical kinetics, the frequency of collisions (Z) is defined as the average number of collisions between particles per unit of time. Assuming all metal atoms have the same average speed at a constant temperature, based on Figure 2, in which element would the collision frequency more likely be higher?

   F. Lithium, because the Li atoms, on average, travel longer distances between consecutive collisions and therefore collide less often.

   G. Lithium, because the Li atoms, on average, travel shorter distances between consecutive collisions and therefore collide more often.

   H. Rubidium, because the Rb atoms, on average, travel longer distances between consecutive collisions and therefore collide less often.

   J. Rubidium, because the Rb atoms, on average, travel shorter distances between consecutive collisions and therefore collide more often.

Passage III

With advances in medicine and nutrition, human life expectancy continues to increase from generation to generation. As human life expectancy increases, new discoveries concerning physical aging are in demand. World human life expectancy has been increasing with each generation since the Middle Ages. Accordingly, scientists are motivated to investigate and better understand the physical aging process, which largely remains a mystery.

Four scientists propose ideas to explain human life expectancy and the physical aging process.

Scientist 1

Human life expectancy is predetermined by our mitochondrial DNA code. In order for cells to replicate, they require energy in the form of ATP to complete the process. As we age, the amount of times our cells can replicate reaches a physical limit due to the deterioration of mitochondria. Once this limit is reached, life is no longer sustainable.

Scientist 2

Human life expectancy is predetermined by our nuclear DNA code. This leads to a process called *apoptosis*, which is a "programmed cell death". After a cell receives the stimulus to undergo degradation, the cell shrinks and all remnants of DNA and RNA decay rapidly. The timing of this stimulus is built into the nuclear DNA code. Once the programmed cell death stimulus is released, life is no longer sustainable.

Scientist 3

Physical aging is the result of DNA damage accumulating throughout the lifespan of the organism. Metabolic processes release compounds that damage DNA, such as *oxygen ions* and *peroxides*. Free radicals attached to these compounds seek stabilization. During stabilization, subatomic particles are removed erroneously from nearby molecules and cause permanent DNA damage. This damage reaches a certain threshold over time beyond which life is no longer sustainable.

Scientist 4

Physical aging is the result of random DNA mutation. Mutations happen periodically throughout the lifetime of an organism and are caused by DNA damage which is not repaired. As DNA damage accumulates, random mutations occur more frequently and eventually lead to a complete denaturing of the genetic code. After the genetic code has denatured, cells are devoid of the ability to replicate and life is no longer sustainable.

13. How does Scientist 3's idea differ from Scientist 4's idea? Scientist 3 proposes that physical aging is the result of:
   A. accumulation of DNA damage, whereas Scientist 4 proposes that physical aging is the result of random DNA mutation caused by DNA damage.
   B. random DNA mutation, whereas Scientist 4 proposes that physical aging is the result of random DNA mutation caused by DNA damage.
   C. accumulation of DNA damage, whereas Scientist 4 proposes that physical aging is the result of DNA damage caused by random DNA mutation.
   D. random DNA mutation, whereas Scientist 4 proposes that physical aging is the result of random DNA mutation caused by DNA damage.

14. Based on the passage, would Scientist 2 or 4 be more likely to argue that the aging of an organism is already programmed at birth?
   F. Scientist 2, because according to Scientist 2, human life expectancy is predetermined by DNA code.
   G. Scientist 2, because according to Scientist 2, aging is the result of random DNA mutation.
   H. Scientist 4, because according to Scientist 4, human life expectancy is predetermined by DNA code.
   J. Scientist 4, because according to Scientist 4, aging is the result of random DNA mutation.

15. Suppose it were discovered that apoptosis has no bearing on human life expectancy. What impact, if any, would this discovery have on Scientist 4's viewpoint?
   A. It would prove that Scientist 4's viewpoint is correct.
   B. It would strengthen Scientist 4's viewpoint, but not prove it is correct.
   C. It would weaken Scientist 4's viewpoint and prove it incorrect.
   D. It would have no impact on Scientist 4's viewpoint.

16. Scientist 2's model would be most weakened if which of the following discoveries were made?

   F. DNA damage accumulates throughout the lifetime of an organism.

   G. Human life expectancy can be calculated to a certain degree at birth.

   H. Human life expectancy is based on random environmental factors.

   J. DNA mutations have no effect on human life expectancy

17. All four scientists would most likely agree with which of the following statements?

   A. An organism eventually reaches a certain point where life is no longer sustainable.

   B. DNA damage directly influences the physical aging process.

   C. DNA mutations have no influence on the physical aging process.

   D. Human life expectancy is a function of genetic code and environmental stimuli.

18. Assume *antioxidants* help slow down the human aging process by safely removing free oxygen radicals that cause DNA damage. This notion helps support the viewpoints of which scientist(s)?

   F. Scientist 3 only

   G. Scientists 2 and 3

   H. Scientists 3 and 4

   J. Scientists 2, 3, and 4

19. According to Scientist 3, which of the following compounds would most likely cause DNA damage?

   A. H_2O

   B. H_2O_2

   C. CH_4

   D. HCl

Passage IV

To increase the quantity of lima beans (*P. lunatus*), farmers experimented with different types of fertilizer: NP, PK, and NPK. NP fertilizers contain nitrogen (N) and phosphorus (P). PK fertilizers contain phosphorus (P) and potassium (K). NPK fertilizers contain nitrogen (N), phosphorus (P), and potassium (K). The farmers set up a study to compare the new types of fertilizer to a normal fertilizer. If the new fertilizer increased the quantity of lima beans above normal levels, the fertilizer was said to be *active*. If a new fertilizer failed to increase the quantity of lima beans above normal levels, the fertilizer was said to be *dormant*.

Study 1

The farmers used 20 lima bean fields and sprayed the top 10 cm of soil with fertilizer NP. During the first day of the study, the soil was left to dry in the sun for 24 hours. Typical conditions were given to the fields to promote lima bean growth. At the end of 30 days the quantity of viable lima beans from each field was recorded. This data was plotted against historical lima bean data utilizing a normal fertilizer for each field. The results of the study are shown in Figure 1.

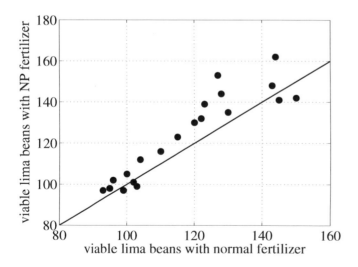

Figure 1

Study 2

The procedure from Study 1 was repeated, except with fertilizer PK. The results of the study are shown in Figure 2.

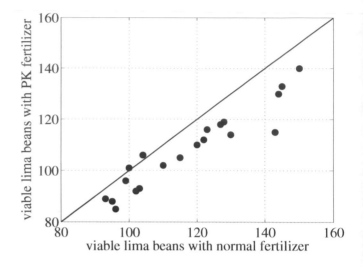

Figure 2

Study 3

The procedure from Study 1 was repeated, except with fertilizer NPK. The results of the study are shown in Figure 3.

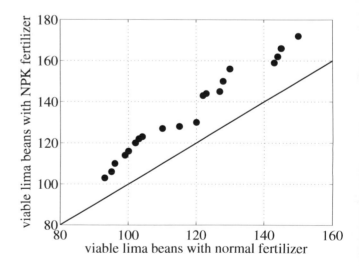

Figure 3

20. According to Figure 1, the NP fertilizer produced approximately how many more viable lima beans when the normal fertilizer produced 120 viable lima beans?
    F. 10 lima beans
    G. 20 lima beans
    H. 30 lima beans
    J. 40 lima beans

21. Based on the results of Studies 1 and 2, which fertilizer, NP or PK, produced more viable lima beans, on average, than the normal fertilizer?
    A. The NP fertilizer, because, on average, there were more viable lima beans than with normal fertilizer.
    B. The NP fertilizer, because, on average, there were less viable lima beans than with normal fertilizer.
    C. The PK fertilizer, because, on average, there were more viable lima beans than with normal fertilizer.
    D. The PK fertilizer, because, on average, there were less viable lima beans than with normal fertilizer.

22. Based on the description of the studies, the purpose of the procedure conducted on the first day was to remove unwanted:
    F. moisture.
    G. organic matter.
    H. *P. lunatus* lima beans.
    J. debris.

23. For all fields tested, the farmers ensured that all other parameters, besides the variables of the experiment, did not change in value. Based on the results of Studies 1-3, which parameters did not change in value between the fields during each of the studies?
    A. The type of fertilizer used and the ambient air temperature
    B. The type of fertilizer used and the amount of precipitation
    C. The ambient air temperature and the amount of precipitation
    D. All parameters were held constant throughout the study.

24. Based on the results of the studies and other information provided, which fertilizers could be considered active?
    F. Fertilizers NP and PK
    G. Fertilizers PK and NPK
    H. Fertilizers NP and NPK
    J. Fertilizers NP, PK, and NPK

25. *Synergy* is the cooperation of two or more components to produce a combined effect greater than the sum of their separate effects. Based on the results of Studies 1-3, do the elements nitrogen, potassium, and phosphorous have synergy with one another in producing more viable lima beans?
    A. No; The results of Studies 1-2 show that when two elements are used, more viable lima beans are produced.
    B. No; The results of Studies 1-2 show that when two elements are used, less viable lima beans are produced.
    C. Yes; The result of Study 3 shows that when all three elements are used together, more viable lima beans are produced.
    D. Yes; The result of Study 3 shows that when all three elements are used together, less viable lima beans are produced.

26. A student hypothesized that fertilizers containing *nonmetal* elements are more active than fertilizers containing *metallic* elements. Do the results of Studies 1 and 2 support this claim?
    F. Yes; The fertilizer from Study 2 contained a metal and yielded more viable lima beans than Study 1, which did not contain a metal.
    G. Yes; The fertilizer from Study 2 contained a metal and yielded less viable lima beans than Study 1, which did not contain a metal.
    H. No; The fertilizer from Study 2 contained a metal and yielded more viable lima beans than Study 1, which did not contain a metal.
    J. No; The fertilizer from Study 2 contained a metal and yielded less viable lima beans than Study 1, which did not contain a metal.

Passage V

A team of three 1900s scientists researched the building blocks of matter. They discovered matter is made up of different elementary particles. The team named the particles *crews* and *leptons*. There were six "flavors" of crews discovered. Three crews in composition make up a *trio*. The most notable trios are the neutron and proton. Electrons, which are the other known major component of the atom, are leptons. Leptons are elementary, half-integer spin particles. There are two major classes of leptons: charged (*electron-like*) and neutral (*neutrinos*).

Table 1 lists the symbol, makeup, and mass of 10 trios discovered by the scientists.

Table 1			
Trios	Symbol	Makeup	Mass (MeV)
Neutron	n	ssd	1,000
Sigma-plus	Σ^+	ddt	1,190
Sigma-zero	Σ^0	dst	1,192
Sigma-minus	Σ^-	sst	1,197
Delta-plus	Δ^+	dds	1,230
Delta-zero	Δ^0	dss	1,230
Delta-minus	Δ^-	sss	1,230
Omega	Ω	ttt	1,700
top Lambda	Λ_t	dsc	n/a*
Proton	p	dds	1,000
*unobservable particle because the cas-crew decays too rapidly			

Table 2 lists the symbol, charge, and mass of 5 leptons discovered by the scientists.

Table 2			
Lepton	Symbol	Charge	Mass (MeV)
Electron	e^-	-1	0.5
Pan	ρ^-	-1	100
Mar	μ^-	-1	175
Ryn	σ^-	-1	825
Lev	λ^-	-1	1,800

Table 3 lists the symbol, charge, and mass of the 6 flavors of crews discovered by the scientists.

Table 3			
Crews	Symbol	Charge	Mass (MeV)
Dag	d	$+2/3$	2.5
Soh	s	$-1/3$	5.0
Hnz	h	$+2/3$	1300
Tlo	t	$-1/3$	100
Cas	c	$+2/3$	170,000
Brg	b	$-1/3$	4,200

27. According to Table 2 and other information provided, the 5 leptons listed belong to which class(es) of leptons?
    A. All 5 leptons listed belong to the charged, electron-like, class.
    B. All 5 leptons listed belong to the neutral, neutrinos, class.
    C. Some leptons listed belong to the charged, electron-like class, and others listed belong to the neutral, neutrinos, class.
    D. Some listed cannot be classified based on the information provided.

28. A physics student predicted that the mass of a proton is calculated by adding the masses of the three crews of which it is composed. Do the results of Table 1 and Table 3 support this prediction?
    F. Yes; The mass of the proton equals the sum of the three crews of its makeup.
    G. Yes; The mass of the proton does not equal the sum of the three crews of its makeup.
    H. No; The mass of the proton equals the sum of the three crews of its makeup.
    J. No; The mass of the proton does not equal the sum of the three crews of its makeup.

29. Do the data in Tables 1 and 3 agree with the known charge of the neutron?
    A. Yes, because Tables 1 and 3 show that the neutron has a charge of 0.
    B. Yes, because Tables 1 and 3 show that the neutron has a charge of +1.
    C. No, because Tables 1 and 3 show that the neutron has a charge of 0.
    D. No, because Tables 1 and 3 show that the neutron has a charge of +1.

30. Based on Tables 1 and 3, the Δ^- trio has the same charge as which other trio listed?
    F. Proton
    G. Neutron
    H. Σ^0
    J. Ω

31. A cas-crew is known to rapidly decay into a brg-crew. Based on this information and Table 1, what will be the total charge of the Λ_t trio after the cas-crew decays?
    A. $-1/3$
    B. 0
    C. $+1/3$
    D. $+2/3$

32. Suppose a physics student wanted to obtain a neutral charge of 0 by combining a pan-lepton, ρ^-, with a trio. Based on Tables 2 and 3, a trio containing which of the following crew combinations would the student choose?
    F. dcb
    G. stb
    H. sht
    J. htb

33. The element *helium*, He, has an atomic number of 2, is electrically neutral, and contains the same number of protons, electrons, and neutrons. Based on Tables 1 and 2, what is the total mass, in MeV, of the elementary particles in helium?
    A. 2,000 MeV
    B. 2,001 MeV
    C. 4,000 MeV
    D. 4,001 MeV

Passage VI

Osmosis is the net movement of water through a semi-permable membrane (such as a cell membrane). During osmosis, H_2O flows from an area of low solute concentration to an area of high solute concentration. Small molecules, such as water, are able to pass through the membrane freely. Large molecules, such as salts and sugars, are too large to pass through the membrane freely. Biology students conducted three experiments to study the process of osmosis.

Experiment 1

0.02 g of NaCl were added to 100 mL of pure H_2O to create a 0.2 g/L solution. A 0.4 g/L, 0.6 g/L, 0.8 g/L, and 1.0 g/L solution were made similarly. The solutions were placed inside of bags composed of polyamide (a material that is permeable to water and impermeable to salt ions and sugars). Excess air was removed from each bag and the bags were sealed tight. The initial mass of each bag and its contents was measured. The bags were placed into separate beakers containing pure H_2O at room temperature, 25°C, for 4 hours. Each bag was removed and the final mass of the bag and its contents was measured. The results of the experiment are shown in Table 1.

Table 1			
Solution (g/L)	Initial mass (g)	Final mass (g)	Difference in mass (g)
0.2	102	121	+19
0.4	104	128	+24
0.6	106	133	+27
0.8	108	137	+29
1.0	110	141	+31

Experiment 2

A teacher handed the students four unknown solutions. Three of the unknown solutions contained a sugar-water mixture and one of the unknown solutions contained a NaCl-water mixture. The solutions were placed inside of polyamide bags. Excess air was removed from each bag and the bags were sealed tight. The initial mass of each bag and its contents was measured. The bags were placed into separate beakers containing pure H_2O at room temperature, 25°C, for 4 hours. Each bag was removed and the final mass of the bag and its contents was measured. The results of the experiment are shown in Table 2.

Table 2			
Solution (g/L)	Initial mass (g)	Final mass (g)	Difference in mass (g)
M	105.2	149.8	+44.6
N	113.5	168.2	+54.7
O	108.4	157.0	+48.6
P	102.5	122.0	+19.5

Experiment 3

The students hypothesized one of the solutions from Experiment 2 to be the NaCl-water mixture and seperated it into five different polyamide bags. The bags were placed in each solution used in Experiment 1. After measuring the final mass of each bag, the students found the final mass increased for four of the trials, but decreased for one of the trials.

34. According to Table 1, as the concentration of the solution increased, the final mass of the polyamide bag that was measured:
    F. increased only.
    G. decreased only.
    H. varied, but with no general trend.
    J. remained constant.

35. Suppose that in Experiment 1 the students had tested a solution with a concentration of 0.7 g/L. Based on the results of Experiment 1, the differnce in mass would most likely have been between:
    A. 19 and 24 grams.
    B. 24 and 27 grams.
    C. 27 and 29 grams.
    D. 29 and 31 grams.

36. If the students wanted to create a 0.5 g/L solution, based on the description of Experiment 1, the students most likely would mix which of the following?
    F. 0.05 g of NaCl with 5 mL of pure H_2O
    G. 0.05 g of NaCl with 100 mL of pure H_2O
    H. 5 g of NaCl with 5 mL of pure H_2O
    J. 5 g of NaCl with 100 mL of pure H_2O

37. Based on the results of the experiments, which unknown solution in Experiment 2 most likely contained the NaCl-water mixture?
    A. Solution M
    B. Solution N
    C. Solution O
    D. Solution P

38. Before the results of the experiments were recorded, one of the students hypothesized that the solutions with relatively more solute would result in a smaller difference in initial to final mass than solutions with relatively less solute. Do the results of the experiments support this hypothesis?
    F. Yes; According to Table 1, the solution with the highest initial mass yielded the greatest difference in mass.
    G. Yes; According to Table 1, the solution with the lowest initial mass yielded the greatest difference in mass.
    H. No; According to Table 1, the solution with the highest initial mass yielded the greatest difference in mass.
    J. No; According to Table 1, the solution with the lowest initial mass yielded the greatest difference in mass.

39. In Experiment 1, which of the following parameters was intentionally varied to explore the process of osmosis?
    A. Solution concentration (g/L)
    B. The molecule of salt
    C. Difference in mass (g)
    D. The material of each bag

40. In biology, the *extracellular fluid*, or fluid outside of cells, typically has a higher solute concentration than *intracellular fluid*, or fluid inside of cells. Based on the passage, how would the transport of particles behave through a cell membrane between extracellular and intracellular fluid?
    F. Salts and sugars would exit the cell through the cell membrane.
    G. Salts and sugars would enter the cell through the cell membrane.
    H. Water would exit the cell through the cell membrane.
    J. Water would enter the cell through the cell membrane.

CHAPTER 7

Putting It All Together: Practice Test 2

SCIENCE

35 Minutes—40 Questions

DIRECTIONS: There are six passages in this test. Each passage is followed by several questions. After reading a passage, choose the best answer to each question and fill in the corresponding oval on your answer document. You may refer to the passages as often as necessary.

You are NOT permitted to use a calculator on this test.

Passage I

A *pedigree chart* is a visual representation of the frequency and appearance of phenotypes of a particular gene. The figure below shows a pedigree chart for red-green color blindness in a human family. The disorder (X⁻) is sex-linked recessive. Since the genes for the red and green color receptors are located on the X chromosome, males are more likely to be affected than females.

Typically, each individual in a pedigree chart is assigned a number. The genotype for Individual 1 is X⁻Y, the genotype for Individual 4 is XX⁻, and the genotype for Individual 24 is X⁻X⁻.

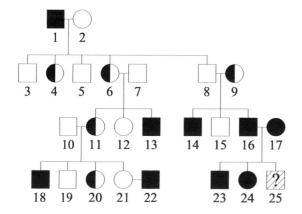

1. Based on the pedigree chart, which of the following pairs of individuals most likely have the most similar genetic information?
   A. Individuals 3 and 5
   B. Individuals 5 and 7
   C. Individuals 4 and 9
   D. Individuals 7 and 23

2. According to the information provided, what is the genotype of Individual 6?
   F. XX
   G. XX⁻
   H. X⁻X⁻
   J. X⁻Y

3. Suppose Individuals 21 and 22 have only male biological children. Based on the pedigree chart, on average, what percent of the children are color blind?
   A. 0 %
   B. 25 %
   C. 50 %
   D. 100 %

4. According to the pedigree chart, and other information provided, is Individual 20 color blind?
   F. Yes, because color blindness is a dominant trait.
   G. Yes, because color blindness is a recessive trait.
   H. No because color blindness is a dominant trait.
   J. No, because color blindness is a recessive trait.

5. A biology student, when looking at the pedigree chart, proposed that Individual 25 would have the genotype XY. Does the information provided support this claim?

A. Yes, because a color blind mother is sufficient to conclude all male biological children will also be color blind.

B. Yes, because a color blind father is sufficient to conclude all male biological children will also be color blind.

C. No, because a color blind mother is sufficient to conclude all male biological children will also be color blind.

D. No, because a color blind father is sufficient to conclude all male biological children will also be color blind.

6. Suppose a female carrier for red-green color blindness had 4 biological children with a normal vision male. How many of the offspring, on average, would be color blind?

F. 0

G. 1

H. 2

J. Cannot be determined from the given information

Passage II

Introduction

Broiler litter (an organic matter) has excellent fertilizing value. Graduate students set up 2 studies to test the efficacy of broiler litter on different plant species: *Persea americana* (avocado) and *Solanum melongena* (eggplant). The students defined *plant yield* as the mass of fruit produced per plant.

Five composites (Composites 1-5) of broiler litter and soil were prepared as specified in Table 1.

	Table 1	
Composite	Broiler litter (%)	Soil (%)
1	0	100
2	25	75
3	50	50
4	75	25
5	100	0

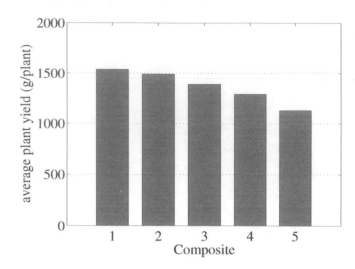

Figure 1

Study 1

Twenty five samples were prepared by placing equal amounts of Composites 1-5 into each pot. 2 kg of Composite 1 were placed into samples 1-5, 2 kg of Composite 2 were placed into samples 6-10, 2 kg of Composite 3 were placed into samples 11-15, and so on. Then, the students added 5 *Persea americana* seeds to each of the 25 samples. The samples were exposed to the same environmental conditions for the next 100 days. On Day 100, the average plant yield of all surviving plants was calculated. The results are shown in Figure 1.

Study 2

The procedure from Study 1 was repeated, except 10 *Solanum melongena* seeds were added to each of the 25 samples instead of *Persea americana* seeds. The samples were exposed to the same environmental conditions for the next 150 days. On Day 150, the average plant yield of all surviving plants was calculated. The results study are shown in Figure 2.

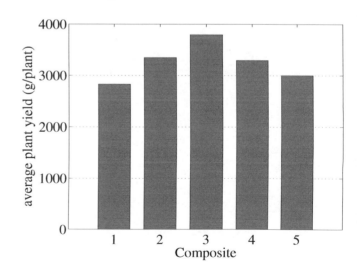

Figure 2

7. Based on Table 1 and Figure 2, as the soil percentage decreased from 100% to 0%, the average plant yield:
   A. increased only.
   B. decreased only.
   C. increased, then decreased.
   D. decreased, then increased.

8. Suppose that, in Study 2, the students calculated the average plant yield in *kilograms* per plant (kg/plant) instead of grams per plant (g/plant). According to Figure 2, the average plant yield for Composite 5 would have been:
   F. 0.3 kg/plant.
   G. 3 kg/plant
   H. 30 kg/plant
   J. 3000 kg/plant.

9. One of the students, before attempting the study, hypothesized that eggplants require a high percentage of broiler litter in the composite to achieve a high average plant yield. Do Table 1 and the results of Study 2 support this hypothesis?
   A. Yes; the highest average plant yield was produced in Composite 3, which had the highest percentage of broiler litter.
   B. Yes; the highest average plant yield was produced in Composite 3, which did NOT have the highest percentage of broiler litter.
   C. No; the highest average plant yield was produced in Composite 3, which had the highest percentage of broiler litter.
   D. No; the highest average plant yield was produced in Composite 3, which did NOT have the highest percentage of broiler litter.

10. In both Studies 1 and 2, which of the following composites was most likely intended by the students to serve as the control group?
    F. Composite 1
    G. Composite 2
    H. Composite 3
    J. Composite 5

11. How did the procedure in Study 1 differ from the procedure in Study 2? In Study 1:
    A. avocado seeds were planted for 100 days, but in Study 2 eggplant seeds were planted for 100 days.
    B. eggplant seeds were planted for 100 days, but in Study 2 avocado seeds were planted for 100 days.
    C. avocado seeds were planted for 100 days, but in Study 2 eggplant seeds were planted for 150 days.
    D. eggplant seeds were planted for 150 days, but in Study 2 avocado seeds were planted for 100 days.

12. The average plant yield in Study 2 is generally greater than the average plant yield in Study 1. Which of the following statements gives the most likely reason for this difference?
    F. There were twice as many eggplant seeds used in Study 2 than avocado seeds used in Study 1.
    G. There were twice as many avocado seeds used in Study 1 than eggplant seeds used in Study 2.
    H. Avocado plants, in general, produce more mass per plant of vegetable than eggplants.
    J. Eggplants, in general, produce more mass per plant of vegetable than avocado plants.

13. The fruit produced by both *Persea americana* and *Solanum melongena* primarily contains which of the following compounds?
    A. O_2
    B. CO_2
    C. CH_3OH
    D. $C_6H_{12}O_6$

Passage III

The snake plant (*Sansevieria trifasciata*) and the areca palm (*Dypsis lutescens*) are known to be efficacious oxygen-producing plants. The snake plant typically converts carbon dioxide to oxygen at night, while the areca plam converts carbon dioxide to oxygen during the day. Biology students conducted a study to measure the oxygen emission rate of both species in various ambient conditions.

Study 1

Snake plant leaves were collected and air-dried. A small quantity, approximately 2-5 grams, was placed in a 1 m^3 glass box with a device that measures O_2 concentration (in mg/m^3). The tank was placed outside at 6:00 A.M. and not disturbed for 24 hours. The lid of the tank was closed. The oxygen gas concentration was recorded every 2 hours (see Figure 1).

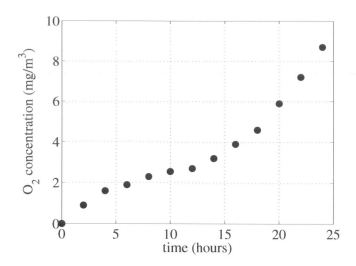

Figure 2

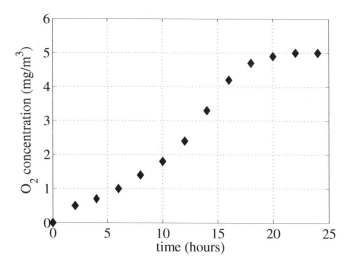

Figure 1

Study 2

The procedure of Study 1 was repeated except that areca palm leaves were tested instead of snake plant leaves (see Figure 2).

Study 3

A small quantity, approximately 2-5 grams, of each species was collected and air-dried. The samples were placed together in a 1 m^3 glass box with a device that measures O_2 concentration (in mg/m^3). The tank was placed outside at 6:00 A.M. and not disturbed for 24 hours. The lid of the tank was closed. The oxygen gas concentration was recorded every 2 hours (see Figure 3).

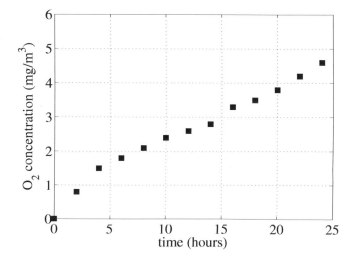

Figure 3

14. According to the results of Study 3, as time elapsed, the O_2 concentration:
   F. increased only.
   G. decreased only.
   H. increased, then decreased.
   J. decreased, then increased.

15. Based on Study 1, at approximately what time did the O_2 concentration of the snake plant leaves reach 2 mg/m^3?
   A. 10:00 A.M.
   B. 12:00 A.M.
   C. 2:00 P.M.
   D. 4:00 P.M.

16. Consider the statement, "When both plant species are placed together, the O_2 concentration is greater at the end of 24 hours than either plant species individually." Do the results of Studies 1-3 support this statement?
   F. Yes; Figure 3 shows a maximum O_2 concentration at the end of 24 hours that is greater than either Figure 1 or Figure 2.
   G. Yes; Figure 1 or 2 shows a maximum O_2 concentration at the end of 24 hours that is greater than Figure 3.
   H. No; Figure 3 shows a maximum O_2 concentration at the end of 24 hours that is greater than either Figure 1 or Figure 2.
   J. No; Figure 1 or 2 shows a maximum O_2 concentration at the end of 24 hours that is greater than Figure 3.

17. Based on Study 1, what was the average O_2 concentration *per leaf* of *Sansevieria trifasciata* after 20 hours had elapsed?
   A. 1 mg/[m^3·leaf]
   B. 5 mg/[m^3·leaf]
   C. 10 mg/[m^3·leaf]
   D. Cannot be determined from the given information

18. What was the most likely reason why the biology students placed the plant samples in boxes made of glass?
   F. To ensure the plant samples received a proper amount of precipitation
   G. To ensure the plant samples receivd a proper amount of sunlight
   H. To protect the plant samples from native herbivores
   J. To protect the plant samples from harmful ultraviolet radiation

19. During which time interval did the O_2 concentration inside of the box containing the snake plant leaves increase *more rapidly* than the O_2 concentration inside of the box containing the areca palm leaves?
   A. 6:00 A.M. - 11:00 A.M.
   B. 4:00 P.M. - 9:00 P.M.
   C. 9:00 P.M. - 2:00 A.M.
   D. 2:00 A.M. - 6:00 A.M.

20. Do the results of Studies 1 and 2 support the introductory information, which states that *Sansevieria trifasciata* typically converts CO_2 to O_2 during the daytime, whereas *Dypsis lutescens* typically converts CO_2 to O_2 during the nighttime?
   F. Yes; For *Sansevieria trifasciata*, the O_2 concentration increased rapidly in the middle of the day, whereas the O_2 concentration for *Dypsis lutescens* increased rapidly at the beginning and end of the day.
   G. Yes; For *Sansevieria trifasciata*, the O_2 concentration decreased rapidly in the middle of the day, whereas the O_2 concentration for *Dypsis lutescens* increased rapidly at the beginning and end of the day.
   H. No; For *Sansevieria trifasciata*, the O_2 concentration increased rapidly in the middle of the day, whereas the O_2 concentration for *Dypsis lutescens* increased rapidly at the beginning and end of the day.
   J. No; For *Sansevieria trifasciata*, the O_2 concentration decreased rapidly in the middle of the day, whereas the O_2 concentration for *Dypsis lutescens* increased rapidly at the beginning and end of the day.

Passage IV

Acid-base indicators, or *pH indicators*, are organic molecules (typically weak acids) that respond to a change in the hydrogen ion (H^+) concentration of a solution. The most common type of pH indicators are ones that change the color of the solution. The pH range where a color change occurs is often referred to as the *transition range*.

Chemistry students attempted to identify the pH of 4 unknown solutions using 4 different pH indicators.

Experiment 1

The students filled 8 clean beakers each with 100 mL of H_2O. Using an pipette, 2 drops of the pH indicator methyl orange were added to 2 of the beakers. This process was repeated for bromthymol blue, phenolphthalein, and bromcresol green. Then, proper amounts of HCl were added to 4 of the beakers, each containing a different indicator, to obtain a pH level of 1-7. The students recorded their observations in Table 1.

(Note: R = red, O = orange, Y = yellow, G = green, B = blue, P = pink, and X = colorless)

Table 1							
pH Indicator	1	2	3	4	5	6	7
Methyl orange	R	R	R	O	Y	Y	Y
Bromthymol blue	Y	Y	Y	Y	Y	Y	G
Phenolphthalein	X	X	X	X	X	X	X
Bromcresol green	Y	Y	Y	G	G	B	B

Experiment 2

Experiment 1 was repeated except proper amounts of NaOH, instead of HCl, were added to the other 4 beakers, each containing a different indicator, to obtain a pH level of 7-13. The students recorded their observations in Table 2.

Table 2							
pH Indicator	7	8	9	10	11	12	13
Methyl orange	Y	Y	Y	Y	Y	Y	Y
Bromthymol blue	G	B	B	B	B	B	B
Phenolphthalein	X	X	P	P	P	P	P
Bromcresol green	B	B	B	B	B	B	B

Experiment 3

The teacher handed the chemistry students 4 solutions (A-D) of unknown pH and 16 clean beakers. The students poured 25 mL of Solution A into 4 of the beakers. Using an pipette, 2 drops of methyl orange were added to one of the 4 beakers. This process was repeated for bromthymol blue, phenolphthalein, and bromcresol green, and then again for Solutions B-D. The students recorded their observations in Table 3.

Table 3				
pH Indicator	A	B	C	D
Methyl orange	Y	Y	O	Y
Bromthymol blue	Y	B	Y	G
Phenolphthalein	X	P	X	X
Bromcresol green	G	B	G	B

21. In Experiment 2, before the addition of NaOH, the pH of the solution was approximately:
    A. 6
    B. 7
    C. 8
    D. 9

22. How did the procedure of Experiment 3 differ from that of Experiment 2? In Experiment 3, the students tested:
    F. only 4 pH indicators, whereas in Experiment 2 more than 4 pH indicators were tested.
    G. only 4 pH indicators, whereas in Experiment 2 less than 4 pH indicators were tested.
    H. solutions of unknown pH, whereas in Experiment 2 students tested solutions of known pH.
    J. solutions of known pH, whereas in Experiment 2 students tested solutions of unknown pH.

23. Based on the passage and the results of Study 1, which of the following best describes the transition range of methyl orange?
    A. a pH range of 1.2 - 3.5
    B. a pH range of 3.3 - 5.1
    C. a pH range of 5.5 - 6.8
    D. a pH range of 7.2 - 8.1

24. A chemist has 2 solutions, one with pH = 5 and the other with pH =11. Based on the results of the experiments, would phenolphthalein be a good pH indicator to use to differentiate the 2 solutions?
    F. Yes, because phenolphthalein is colorless at both pH = 5 and pH = 11.
    G. No, because phenolphthalein is colorless at pH = 5 and pink at pH = 11.
    H. No, because phenolphthalein is colorless at both pH = 5 and pH = 11.
    J. Yes, because phenolphthalein is colorless at pH = 5 and pink at pH = 11.

25. At the conclusion of the experiments, one of the students concluded that the pH of Solution A was between 3-4. Do the results of Experiments 1-3 support this conclusion?
    A. Yes, because in Solution A methyl orange was yellow.
    B. Yes, because in Solution A bromthymol blue was yellow.
    C. No, because in Solution A methyl orange was yellow.
    D. No, because in Solution A bromthymol blue was yellow.

26. The teacher informed the class that the pH of one of the unknown solutions could not be determined given the 4 pH indicators chosen for the experiments. Based on the results of Experiments 1-3, which unknown solution was it?
    F. Solution A
    G. Solution B
    H. Solution C
    J. Solution D

27. In chemistry, the pOH (the measure of the concentration of the OH^- ion) and the pH of a solution always add to 14. Based on this information, and the results of the experiments, which unknown solution has the *highest* pOH?
    A. Solution A
    B. Solution B
    C. Solution C
    D. Solution D

Passage V

A physics teacher described the following theoretical experiment to her class.

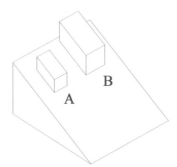

Figure 1

Object A and Object B, with masses 10 kg and 20 kg respectively, are released from rest from the top of a frictionless inclined plane (see Figure 1). The only force acting on each object is the force due to gravity, F_g. The acceleration due to gravity on Earth, g, is constant ($g = 9.8$ m/s^2). The time it takes for each object to reach the bottom of the inclined plane is recorded.

The teacher asks 3 students to predict which object will reach the bottom of the inclined plane first and to support their claim using their understanding of physics.

Student 1

Object A will reach the bottom of the inclined plane first because lighter objects move faster. Since the force of gravity is constant near the surface of the Earth, the object with less mass will experience a greater average speed down the inclined plane. This is evident in other experiments as well. For example, an average human pushing a shopping cart will travel faster than the same individual pushing a motor vehicle. Moreover, since both objects need to travel the same distance to reach the bottom, the speed of each object is the only factor worth noting.

Student 2

Object B will reach the bottom of the inclined plane first because heavier objects experience greater momentum. This is evident in the equation $p = mv$, where p is the object's momentum, m is the object's mass, and v is the object's speed. According to this equation, p and m are directly related. Since Object B has twice the mass of Object A, it will also have twice the momentum. It is easier for heavier objects to gain momentum, and thus, gain greater speeds.

Student 3

Objects A and B will reach the bottom of the inclined plane at the exact same time because the gravitational forces acting on both objects are the same. The variable m, which represents the mass of each object, becomes obsolete when correctly manipulating the force equations in the inclined plane experiment. If any physical factors, such as friction, are unequally distributed on the surface of the inclined plane, it will result in a difference in fall time between the objects. However, since the inclined plane is frictionless we need not worry about these terms in the equations. Moreover, because both objects are starting from the same height above the bottom of the inclined plane, the recorded times to reach the bottom will be identical.

28. According to Student 1, as the mass of an object increases, the average speed of that object traveling down the inclined plane:
    F. increases.
    G. decreases.
    H. varies, but with no general trend.
    J. remains constant.

29. Suppose a bowling ball and a baseball are dropped from the same height above the surface of Earth. Would Student 1 or Student 2 more likely argue that the bowling ball would fall and reach the surface of the Earth before the baseball?
    A. Student 1, because Student 1 argues that lighter objects travel faster than heavier objects.
    B. Student 1, because Student 1 argues that lighter objects travel slower than heavier objects.
    C. Student 2, because Student 2 argues that lighter objects travel faster than heavier objects.
    D. Student 2, because Student 2 argues that lighter objects travel slower than heavier objects.

30. Which of the student(s) would agree that the *acceleration* of the object varies with the object's mass?
    F. Student 1 only
    G. Student 2 only
    H. Students 1 and 2
    J. Students 2 and 3

31. The force due to gravity on Earth, F_g, of an object is equal to the mass of the object times g. According to the information provided, which of the following is closest to the force due to gravity of Object A?

   A. 100 N

   B. 200 N

   C. 300 N

   D. 400 N

32. Assume the inclined plane had an equal distribution of friction on its surface. According to Student 3, how would the time it takes to reach the bottom of the inclined for Object A compare to Object B? The fall time of Object A would be:

   F. twice as great as the fall time of Object B.

   G. equal to the fall time of Object B.

   H. half as great as the fall time of Object B.

   J. one-fourth as great as the fall time of Object B.

33. Two new similar objects, Object C and Object D, are introduced into the same theoretical experiment. Object D is known to have a greater mass than Object C. A fourth student predicts that Object C will reach the bottom of the inclined plane first. Which student, if any, would agree with the prediction stated by the fourth student?

   A. Student 1

   B. Student 2

   C. Student 3

   D. None of the students

34. *Newton's second law* states that the force of an object equals the mass of that object multiplied by its acceleration. Based on Student 3's argument, how would the acceleration of Object A compare to the acceleration of Object B? The acceleration of Object A would be:

   F. less, because Object A has a greater mass than Object B.

   G. less, because Object B has a greater mass than Object A.

   H. greater, because Object B has a greater mass than Object A.

   J. equal to the acceleration of Object B.

Passage VI

A *double-slit experiment* demonstrates that light simultaneously exhibits properties of both a wave and a particle. In the demonstration, a wave is split into two separate waves that later combine into a single wave. This creates an *interference pattern*, producing both bright and dark bands on a screen. An interference pattern would not take place if light consisted only of particles. Furthermore, light is known to travel only through one slit and not both. This is a property of particles, whereas waves would travel through both slits.

Physics students constructed 3 double-slit experiments to better understand how various parameters affect the distance between bands on the screen.

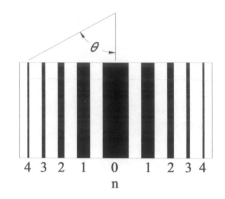

Figure 2

Experiment 1

A monochromatic light source, producing a wavelength (λ) of 625 nm, was placed on a platform. Scissors were used to cut 2 vertical parallel slits, a distance $d = 0.1$ cm apart, through a flat piece of paper. The paper was positioned at the same height as the light source so that the light beam precisely hit both slits. Another piece of paper was positioned a distance $L = 10$ m away from the two slits (see Figure 1).

Table 1		
Trial	d (cm)	x (cm)
1	0.1	2.50
2	0.2	1.25
3	0.3	0.83

Experiment 2

The procedure from Experiment 1 was repeated for various values of L (see Table 2). Each trial had a d of 0.1 cm and a λ of 625 nm.

Table 2		
Trial	L (m)	x (cm)
4	20	5.0
5	30	7.5
6	40	10.0

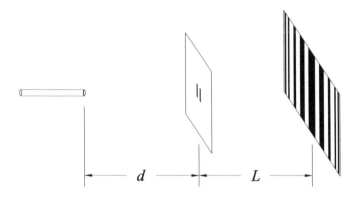

Figure 1

All sources of external light were blocked from entering the room. The monochromatic light source was turned on, producing a double-slit band pattern on the far piece of paper (see Figure 2). The students highlighted the double-slit band pattern with pencil. The distance, x, between the center band (n = 0) and the 4th band (n = 4) was recorded. The experiment was repeated for various values of d and the results recorded in Table 1.

Experiment 3

The procedure from Experiment 1 was repeated for various wavelengths of monochromatic light (see Table 3). Each trial had a d of 0.1 cm and a L of 10 m.

Table 3		
Trial	λ (nm)	x (cm)
7	650	2.6
8	700	2.8
9	750	3.0

35. If, in Experiment 2, a trial had been conducted in which L equaled 60 m, x would most likely have been closest to which of the following values?
    A. 8.75 cm
    B. 10.0 cm
    C. 12.5 cm
    D. 15.0 cm

36. In Experiment 1, which of the following is the most likely reason why the students blocked all sources of natural light from entering the room?
    F. To better see the double-slit band pattern
    G. To avoid other sources of light causing unnecessary interference
    H. To remove excess heat from the room
    J. To ensure the laboratory setup would not be disturbed

37. In Experiment 1, which variable was independent, and which variable was dependent?

	independent	dependent
A.	L	λ
B.	d	λ
C.	L	x
D.	d	x

38. Suppose that the procedure used in Trial 7 had been repeated in a new trial, except L equaled 5 m. Based on the results of Experiments 2 and 3, x would most likely have been:
    F. less than 2.6 cm.
    G. between 2.6 cm and 2.8 cm.
    H. between 2.8 cm and 3.0 cm.
    J. greater than 3.0 cm.

39. Based on the results of the experiments, which of the following equations correctly relates x to d, L, and λ?
    (Note: k is an unknown constant.)
    A. $x = k\dfrac{L}{d\lambda}$
    B. $x = k\dfrac{Ld}{\lambda}$
    C. $x = k\dfrac{L\lambda}{d}$
    D. $x = k\dfrac{\lambda}{Ld}$

40. Based on the procedure used in Trial 3 and Figure 2, which of the following equations gives the *angle of elevation*, θ, measured from the center of the two slits to the 4th band (n = 4) on the interference pattern?
    F. $\theta = \sin^{-1}\left(\dfrac{0.83}{10}\right)$
    G. $\theta = \sin^{-1}\left(\dfrac{0.83}{1,000}\right)$
    H. $\theta = \tan^{-1}\left(\dfrac{0.83}{10}\right)$
    J. $\theta = \tan^{-1}\left(\dfrac{0.83}{1,000}\right)$

CHAPTER 8

ANSWERS AND EXPLANATIONS

8.1   Chapter Questions

CHAPTER ONE	CHAPTER TWO	CHAPTER THREE	CHAPTER FOUR
1.2	**2.1**	**3.1**	**4.1**
1. A	1. C	1. C	1. A
2. J	2. H	2. J	2. H
3. D	3. B	3. A or B	3. A
	4. J	4. F	
1.3	5. A	5. B	**4.2**
4. F		6. J	4. J
5. A	**2.2**		5. A
6. G	6. J		6. J
7. D	7. B		
8. F	8. G		**4.3**
9. B	9. D		7. D
10. F			8. H
11. A	**2.3**		9. C
12. J	10. J		10. J
13. B	11. C		11. A
14. G	12. J		12. J
	13. D		13. C
1.4			
15. B	**2.4**		
m1. 20	14. G		
m2. 140	15. B		
m3. 300	16. H		
m4. 5			
m5. 140	**2.5**		
m6. 1,200	17. C		
m7. 2,000	18. F		
m8. 550	19. A		CHAPTER FIVE
m9. 3	20. H		**5.1**
m10. 720			1. A
m11. 25	**2.6**		2. J
m12. 1,000	21. D		3. C
m13. 600	22. H		
m14. 6,000	23. D		**5.2**
	24. F		4. G
1.5			5. A
16. J			6. H
17. D			
18. J			**5.1**
19. D			7. B
20. F			8. G
			9. B
1.6			
21. D			
22. G			
23. C			
24. F			
25. C			
26. G			

8.2   Chapter 1 Test: The Basics

#	ANSWER	SKILL	EXPLANATION
1	A	Locators	The lowest time to reach the medium implies the stimulus is most effective.
2	F	Number Behavior	Table 3 shows a direct trend between stimulus introduced and time to reach medium.
3	D	Locators	The results of Study 1 show shorter times than Study 2. This implies normal cockroaches complete the maze faster than abnormal cockroaches. The acetic acid stimulus, according to Table 2, results in a slower time than lemon oil.
4	H	Number Behavior	According to Table 3, a new data point of 7% would result in a time between 27 and 48 seconds.
5	B	Math	The time for lemon oil in Table 2 is 30 seconds. Conversion to minutes yields $1/2$ or 0.50 minutes.
6	J	Number Behavior	Table 3 shows a direct trend. Using this trend for ethanol, and the result for ethanol in Table 1 of 18 seconds, an increase in ethanol concentration would result in a longer time to reach the medium.
7	B	Number Behavior	Comparing Table 1 and Table 2, the abormal cockroaches have longer times for all stimuli than the normal cockroaches. Since Study 3 repeated the procedure from Study 1, which used normal cockroaches, using abnormal cockroaches instead would yield longer times for all stimuli.
8	G	Number Behavior	Figure 1 shows an inverse trend between temperature and density.
9	A	Number Behavior	Figure 2 shows a direct trend between temperature and absolute pressure.
10	F	Number Behavior	Figure 3 shows a direct trend between temperature and specific entropy.
11	D	Extrapolation and Estimation	A x-axis value of 130°C would yield a y-axis value much greater than 120 kN/m^2.
12	H	Data Bridge	Given a density of 970 kg/m^3, a value of approximately 82°C is determined from Figure 1. Using that value for temperature in Figure 2 yields an absolute pressure of approximately 50 kN/m^2.
13	C	Extrapolation and Estimation	A x-axis value of 110°C would yield a y-axis value between 1.25 and 1.5 kJ/kg-K.
14	H	Outside Knowledge	Figure 3 best resembles a line.
15	B	Number Behavior	Trials 1 to 3 show an inverse trend with respect to time.
16	G	Number Behavior	Trials 7 to 9 show an inverse trend with respect to time.
17	C	Math	The passage states each object is 2.0 kg. If 5 objects were used then the total weight would be 10 kg.
18	G	Number Behavior	The fastest speed would result from the lowest time to fall down the inclined plane.
19	B	Number Behavior	The new brick surface for a sphere yields a time between Trials 2 and 3. This would be the same for the cube and Trials 5 and 6.
20	J	Cannot Be Determined	The passage does not provide any information about glass objects.

#	Answer	Skill	Explanation
21	A	Number Behavior	Table 1 shows a direct trend between distance and pH.
22	F	Number Behavior	Figure 1 shows a direct trend between days and radiation level for all water sources.
23	A	Number Behavior	Using both Table 1 and Figure 1, as the pH level increases so does the water source number. And as the water source number increases, the radiation level increases.
24	F	Number Behavior	Using both Table 1 and Figure 1, as the distance from the power plant increases so does the water source number. And as the water source number increases, the radiation level increases.
25	D	Extrapolation and Estimation	Based on Figure 1, a x-axis value of 25 days would yield a y-axis value close to 1,000 mG.
26	H	Data Bridge	In Table 1, 27 m is located between water sources 2 and 3. In Figure 1, a x-axis value of 10 days would yield a y-axis value of approximately 625 mG for a water source between sources 2 and 3.
27	A	Number Behavior	Table 1 shows a direct trend between amount of sunlight and final height.
28	F	Number Behavior	Table 2 shows a direct trend between the amount of water per day and final height.
29	B	Number Behavior	Table 3 shows an inverse trend between sunflower number and final height.
30	J	Number Behavior	66 cm is located between 75% and 100% in Table 1, and between 10 mL and 20 mL in Table 2.
31	B	Number Behavior	40% is located between 22 cm and 39 cm in Table 1.
32	G	Math	To convert from centimeters to meters, divide by 100. Because 100 centimeters is exactly 1 meter, Sunflower 5 in Study 2 is closest with a final height of 102 cm.
33	B	Locators	The answer choices tell us to look at Study 3. The description of Study 3 says that 20 mL of water was used. When 20 mL of water was used in Study 2, the final height was 80 cm. Soil type B in Table 3 also yielded a final height of 80 cm.
34	F	Number Behavior	Table 1 shows a direct trend between mass and volume.
35	A	Number Behavior	Table 1 shows a direct trend between mass and surface area.
36	G	Number Behavior	Figure 2 shows an inverse trend between time and temperature.
37	B	Number Behavior	3.1 kg is located between Ball A and Ball B in Table 1.
38	J	Locators	The cooling rate is defined in the description above Figure 2. The slope of a graph is rise/run. In Figure 2, °C is the y-axis (or rise), and minutes is the x-axis (or run).
39	B	Locators	The passage mentions that the freezer is set to 0°C. The temperatures of each sphere will eventually reach the temperature of the freezer.
40	J	Locators	The material of each sphere is a constant in the experiment. It is impossible to determine how using plastic, instead of metal, would change the results.

8.3   Chapter 2 Test: Advanced Question Types

#	Answer	Skill	Explanation
1	A	Number Behavior	Figure 1 shows a direct trend between months elapsed and CO_2 emissions for Source 1.
2	H	Scientific Method	Soil activity is most likely better in months that promote plant growth.
3	B	Yes, Yes, No, No	Since *E. coli* produce NO_2^-, and there is at least some NO_2^- present in all 3 months, then *E. coli* were present.
4	J	Math	Figure 1 gives approximately 20, 40, and 60 mol/cm^3 for months 1, 2, and 3 respectively. The total emissions would be the sum, or approximately 120 mol/cm^3.
5	A	Math	The passage describes the dimensions of the soil section as 1.0 m, 1.0 m, and 3.0 m. The volume, therefore, would be the product of these dimensions, or 3.0 m^3.
6	F	Extrapolation and Estimation	Figure 2 shows an inverse trend between months elapsed and NO_2^- emissions for Source 2. An additional month would yield an even lower value for NO_2^- emissions, leaving Answer F as the best choice.
7	D	Locators	The passage describes anaerobic respiration as the consumption of NO_3^- and production of NO_2^-. Answer D is the only choice with these compounds on the appropriate sides of the chemical equation.
8	F	Number Behavior	Figure 1 shows a direct trend between pH level and bacteria concentration at 20 min.
9	B	Mixing	Figure 2 yields a value of 30 kg/L at 10 min and a value of 20 kg/L at 25 min. The correct answer of a mixing problem will be between the two data points.
10	H	Scatter Plots	In Figure 2, the data is plotted once every 5 minutes.
11	A	Scientific Method	pH is an independent variable in Study 1 but a constant in Study 2. Water temperature is a constant in both studies. Chlorine concentration is a constant in Study 1 but an independent variable in Study 2. Bacteria concentration is the dependent variable in both studies.
12	G	Yes, Yes, No, No	Answer choices H and J have incorrect explanations. The correct explanation disagrees with the hypothesis of the student.
13	D	Cannot Be Determined	The water temperature is constant through the experiment. There is no way of knowing, based on what is giving, how changing this parameter would affect the results.
14	G	Outside Knowledge	Knowledge of the pH scale is needed. Acids have a pH lower than 7. Bases have a pH higher than 7.
15	C	Locators	All y-axis values for CH_4 in Figure 2 are between 0.995 and 1.000.
16	G	Number Behavior	Figure 1 shows an inverse trend between pressure and compressability factor for CO_2.
17	A	Equations as Answer Choices	The best point to test for SF_6 in Figure 1 is (10,0.9). Answer choices B and D can be removed because the slope in Figure 1 is negative. Only Answer A works with the given data point.

#	Answer	Skill	Explanation
18	J	Yes, Yes, No, No	Answer choices F and H have the incorrect explanation. The correct explanation disagrees with the chemist
19	A	Number Behavior	In Figure 2, generally, temperature and compressability factor have a direct relationship. Had Figure 1 been recorded at a lower tempearture, all values of z would also decrease.
20	F	Locators	Based on the equation in the passage, an actual volume that is greater than the ideal volume would yield a value greater than 1. H_2 is the only gas in either Figure 1 or 2 with values greater than 1.
21	C	Locators	The half-life of U-235, according to Table 1, is 7×10^8 yr.
22	J	Yes, Yes, No, No	Answer choices F and H have the incorrect explanation. The correct explanation disagrees with the scientist.
23	C	Locators	If 150 atoms decayed, then 850 remain. A y-axis value of 850 yields a x-axis value of 10×10^8 yr.
24	F	Extrapolation and Estimation	Extending the U-235 line to a x-axis value of 12×10^8 years would yield a y-axis value lower than 400 atoms.
25	B	Data Bridge	Using Table 1, Tc-99 is located between U-233 and U-235. Jumping to Figure 1, the number of atoms, for any given amount of time, will also be between U-233 and U-235.
26	J	Math	Using the equation in the passage, if C-14 has a half-life of 5,715 years, then: $\tau = \dfrac{5,715}{0.7}$. This will yield a value for τ greater than 5,715.
27	A	Number Behavior	Table 1 shows a direct trend between weight and $1/4$-mile time.
28	G	Yes, Yes, No, No	Answer choices F, H, and J have incorrect explanations.
29	B	Locators	A value of 950 cfm, in Table 2, is located between Trials 3 and 4.
30	H	Scientific Method	Based on the description of Study 1, 750 cfm was a constant throughout the study. In Study 2, this value yielded a $1/4$-mile time of 12.3 seconds. The car in Study 1 that also resulted in the same $1/4$-mile time is Car E.
31	D	Scientific Method	Engine horsepower is a constant in Study 1, but the independent variable in Study 3.
32	H	Scientific Method	Based on the description of Study 1, 450 hp was a constant throughout the study. In Study 2, this value yielded a $1/4$-mile time of 9.3 seconds. The car in Study 1 that also resulted in the same $1/4$-mile time is Car C.
33	D	Number Behavior	Table 3 shows an inverse trend between Engine horsepower and $1/4$-mile time. If Engine horsepower is decreased from 450 hp to 300 hp, the $1/4$-mile time will increase. The original $1/4$-mile time for Car E in Study 1 is 12.3 seconds.
34	F	Number Behavior	Figure 2 shows a direct trend between water temperature and survival percentage.
35	C	Locators	Most resistant implies the survival percentage is high. Species C has the highest survival percentage.

#	Answer	Skill	Explanation
36	F	Number Behavior	Table 1 shows a direct trend between the water treatment number and pH level. Figure 2 shows a direct trend between the water treatment level and the survival percentage at a given temperature. Thus, there is a direct trend between the pH level and survival percentage.
37	D	Scientific Method	Water temperature is a constant in Experiment 1 but an independent variable in Experiment 2.
38	G	Yes, Yes, No, No	Answer choices F and H have incorrect explanations. The correct explanation disagrees with the researcher's prediction.
39	B	Scientific Method	The water temperature used in Experiment 1 was 25°C. At this temperature, the results of Species B in Figure 1 best match the results of 25°C in Figure 2.
40	G	Yes, Yes, No, No	Answer choices H and J have incorrect explanations. To promote growth would imply a higher survival percentage. According to Figure 2, as temperature increases so does survival percentage.

8.4 Chapters 3 and 4 Test: Scientific Method and Last Questions

#	Answer	Skill	Explanation
1	D	Cannot Be Determined	Gene Y is present in Cross 1, not Cross 2.
2	F	Math	Approximately 100 out of 400 offspring from Cross 1 were green.
3	D	Outside Knowledge	Recessive phenotypes generally appear less often than dominant phenotypes. Table 1 shows green is a recessive trait and Table 2 shows wrinkled is a recessive trait.
4	F	Outside Knowledge	A double Punnett square here is needed. Answer choice J is wrong because it would have a chance to produce the green phenotype. Answer choices G and H are wrong because those crosses would produce round and wrinkled offspring.
5	C	Math	There are a total of 400 offspring, of which 250 are yellow and round.
6	F	Outside Knowledge	A double Punnett square here is needed. Since both plants are green, only green offspring would result. And since one of the plants is already wrinkled, there is a 0% chance of yielding homozygous dominant offspring for shape.
7	A	Number Behavior	Table 1 shows a direct trend between W and D.
8	G	Number Behavior	A value of 175 N/m^2 would be between Trials 7 and 8 in Table 2.
9	B	Locators	All of the answer choices have a value of 30 N for W. The highest value of D occurs in Trial 5.
10	G	Scientific Method	Study 2 has a constant value for W of 30 N. This value in Study 1 yields a D of 2.5×10^{-3}. That same value for D occurs in Trial 6 using Metal B.

#	Answer	Skill	Explanation
11	A	Number Behavior	Table 1 shows a direct trend between W and D. Table 3 shows a direct trend between T and D. Thus, if the students wanted the lowest extent of deformation, the lowest values for both W and D would be chosen.
12	F	Scientific Method	W is a constant in Study 2 and the independent variable in Study 1.
13	C	Outside Knowledge	"According to the information provided" indicates we must look at the passage. Each pipe has a mass of 10 kg. The force due to gravity is the product of an object's mass times the acceleration due to gravity (which is approximately 10 m/s^2). The result is a weight of 100 N.
14	G	Number Behavior	Figure 3 shows an inverse trend between voltage and resistance.
15	D	Extrapolation and Estimation	Extending the curve for the diode off the chart would yield a current well above 10 mA.
16	F	Number Behavior	In Figure 3, as the resistance decreases the voltage increases. In Figure 2, as the voltage increases the current increases. Hence, as the resistance decreases the current increases.
17	B	Data Bridge	A y-axis value of 5 Ω for the LED in Figure 3 yields a x-axis value of approximately 1.8 V. In Figure 2, this same x-axis value yields a y-axis value of approximately 1.7 mA.
18	H	Scientific Method	"Intentionally varied" implies independent variable. The x-axis and key display independent variables in a figure.
19	D	Yes, Yes, No, No	Answer choices A and C have incorrect explanations. The correct explanation disagrees with the student's statement.
20	F	Inverse Trends	The least amount of electrical current is a result of the greatest resistance. The filament lamp in Figure 3 has the greatest resistance at any given voltage.
21	A	Number Behavior	In increasing order of olivine concentration: D, A, B, then C. This order is also present in Figure 2 with regard to increasing hydrogen concentration.
22	J	Math	The description states the device has a circular radius of 10 m. According to the equation $A = \pi r^2$, this would yield an area of 100π.
23	B	Extrapolation and Estimation	Location B has a hydrogen concentration that is approximately 70 g/m^3 at a depth of 20 m. Based on the curve, the hydrogen concentration would not change by much from 20 m to 25 m.
24	G	Locators	The hydrogen gas concentration of Location B is to the right of Location A at all depths, indicating a higher value.
25	D	Math	At a depth of 20 m, Location B has a hydrogen concentration of approximately 70 g/m^3. If a volume of 10 m^3 is collected, there would have to be 700 grams in order for the concentration to equal 70 g/m^3.
26	G	Mixing	A depth of 15 m for Location D yields a hydrogen concentration of approximately 10 g/m^3. A depth of 15 m for Location A yields a hydrogen concentration of approximately 30 g/m^3. The correct answer for mixing problems is always between the two data points.
27	B	Outside Knowledge	Olivine is Fe_2SiO_4 and magnetite is Fe_3O_4 as described in the passage. According to the chemical equation, doubling the moles of olivine from 3 to 6 would double the moles of magnetite from 2 to 4.

#	ANSWER	SKILL	EXPLANATION
28	H	Data Bridge	Figure 2 shows genotype HH as having the most food searching events per day. Figure 3 shows genotype HH with a maximum age of 50 days.
29	A	Yes, Yes, No, No	Answer choices C and D have incorrect explanations. The correct explanation suggests blow flies with two normal alleles spend more time searching for food than ones with abnormal alleles.
30	H	Math	Figure 2 shows genotype HH with approximately 15 and H⁻H⁻ with approximately 3 food searching events per day. The ratio is 5:1 or 5 times as great.
31	C	Yes, Yes, No, No	Answer choices B and D have incorrect explanations. The correct explanation disagrees with the student's hypothesis.
32	F	Outside Knowledge	A Punnett square is required to determine that all offspring will have the heterozygous genotype. According to Figure 3, genotype HH⁻ has a 0 percent survival rate after 40 days.
33	A	Anticipating the Extra Step	A Punnett square shows that 50% of the offspring will have genotype HH⁻, and the other 50% will have genotype H⁻H⁻. According to Figure 3, the correct answer will fall between 20 days and 35 days, the maximum lifespan of genotypes HH⁻ and H⁻H⁻ respectively.
34	J	Yes, Yes, No, No	Answer choices G and H have incorrect explanations. The heavier mass will experience a greater force due to gravity.
35	A	Math	The spring constant is $k = 100$ N/m. The 250 N force in the question is 2.5 times as great, resulting in 2.5 meters of compression.
36	F	Number Behavior	The mass of the spheres in increasing order are: A, B, then C. This results in an increase in average spring compression according to Table 1.
37	C	Scientific Method	Experiment 3 states that the spring was moved 0.5 m away from the base of the quarter-pipe. In Experiment 2, the initial height, H, is an independent variable.
38	F	Outside Knowledge	All answer explanations are correct. The greatest kinetic energy would yield the largest spring compression. Sphere C, since it is the most massive, would have the greatest amount of kinetic energy.
39	A	Scientific Method	In Table 2, the initial height is intentionally varied while the spring compression is measured.
40	H	Math	The mass of Sphere C is 3 kg, the acceleration due to gravity is 10 m/s², and the initial height is 1 m. Substituting all values into the given equation yields a result of 30 J.

8.5 Chapter 5 Test: Conflicting Viewpoints

#	ANSWER	SKILL	EXPLANATION
1	C	Outside Knowledge	NaCl, or sodium chloride, is a common salt in chemistry.
2	J	Step One	The first sentences of each student show us that Students 2 mentions a charged center and Student 3 agrees with Student 2's viewpoint.
3	C	Step One	Student 1 mentions a rough surface producing friction. This matches the sandpaper mentioned in answer choice C.
4	F	Step One	Although Student 3 deviates from Student 2, they both agree with the notion that the surface of the metal caused the spark.
5	D	Step One	The smooth surface eliminates Student 1. The uncharged surface eliminates Students 2 and 3.
6	H	Step Two	The key phrase in the question is "negative and positive charged particles." Students 2 and 3 argue the charged surface of the metal causes the spark.
7	D	The Irrelevant Argument	It is impossible based on the information given how introducing a different solvent would change the experiment.
8	H	Step One	The first sentences of Scientists 1 and 3 state a positively charged center. Scientists 2 and 4 agree with these statements.
9	B	Step Two	The key phrase in the question is "most massive." Scientist 1 states a larger mass than Scientist 3, eliminating Scientists 3 and 4. The exception stated by Scientist 2 argues a more massive nucleus.
10	G	Step Two	The key term in the question is "density." Scientist 1 states that the nucleus is most dense, "whereas the area outside...is not very dense."
11	D	Step Two	The key phrase in the question is "all protons...are located inside the nucleus." Scientists 3 and 4 mention protons outside of the nucleus. However, Scientist 4 mentions there are an equal amount of protons outside of the nucleoid region, whereas Scientist 3 states that most protons are located inside the nucleoid region.
12	F	Yes, Yes, No, No	The key phrase in the question is "positive particles aggegrate to the center." All Scientists would agree with this statement. Answer choices G and J have incorrect explanations.
13	B	Step Two	The last sentence of Scientist 1 states the neutron has a neutral charge. The only device that relates to "charge" is an electrometer.
14	G	Outside Knowledge	It is known that all protons and neutrons are located within the nucleus, which is stated by Scientist 2.
15	C	Outside Knowledge	Berries are classified under the Plantae kingdom.
16	F	Step One	The opening sentences of each hypothesis are vastly different. Hypothesis 1 mentions "without pausing during flight."
17	C	Step Two	The key phrase of the answer choices is "energy acquired." The last sentence of all 3 hypotheses mention energy being retrieved during flight.

#	Answer	Skill	Explanation
18	F	Yes, Yes, No, No	Hypothesis 1 mentions the break down of muscle cells. Answer choices G and J have incorrect explanations. The correct explanation agrees with the question.
19	B	Step Two	The key phrase of the question is "invertebrate". Hypothesis 2 is the only viewpoint that mentions invertebrates.
20	J	The Irrelevant Argument	The viewpoints are discussing acquisition of energy and how that energy is stored during flight. The discovery in the question is irrelevant.
21	C	Outside Knowledge	ATP, or adenosine triphosphate, is the primary energy carrying molecule found in the cells of all living organisms.
22	J	Step One	First sentences show the genetic code of fibrin is altered in Hypotheses 2 and 3, while the genetic code of prothrombin is altered in Hypotheses 1 and 4.
23	D	Yes, Yes, No, No	Answer choices A and C have incorrect explanations. The correct explanation disagrees with the question.
24	F	Step Two	First sentences show Hypothesis 1 states prothrombin is altered. According to the text, when prothrombin is activated it causes thrombin to form.
25	C	Step Two	The key phrase of the question is "a substance...identical to thrombin." Hypothesis 4 states that "because thrombin is never produced fibrinogen is never converted into fibrin."
26	G	Locators	Hypotheses 1 and 4 both state that "thrombin is never produced." This implies a low concentration of thrombin.
27	B	Step One	First sentences of Hypotheses 2 and 3 state the genetic code of fibrin is altered by hemophilia.
28	G	Outside Knowledge	White blood cells are a component of the immune system.
29	A	Scientific Method	The entire passage is about dissolving a solute into different solvents.
30	H	Step One	The second sentence of Student 3 states the solute "must have been nonpolar."
31	C	Step Two	Student 1 states "the solute...must have also been polar." Student 2 agrees with Student 1.
32	J	Step Two	The last sentence of Student 3 states that nonpolar solvents can dissolve any solute. This disagrees with answer choice J.
33	C	Yes, Yes, No, No	Answer choices B and D have incorrect explanations. According to Student 1 a nonpolar solute would not dissolve in water.
34	G	Outside Knowledge	Table 1 tells us that Ligroin is similar to Toluene, which is a nonpolar solvent. Methane, CH_4, is also nonpolar.
35	A	Step One	First sentences show Graduate Student 1's main argument concerns Earth's gravity.
36	F	Number Behavior	According to the data, Snowboarder A had a kinetic energy at Point X of 0. Because the athletes underwent the same experiment, it can be concluded that Snowboarder B would also have a kinetic energy at Point X of 0. In addition, objects at rest have a value of 0 for kinetic energy.

#	Answer	Skill	Explanation
37	B	Step Two	The main phrase of the question is "2 kg." Graduates Students 1 and 3 both state that "mass...had no effect on the results."
38	J	Yes, Yes, No, No	Answer choices G and H have incorrect explanations. Since the two masses had identical fall times it would weaken Graduate Student 2's viewpoint, who is the only student to argue that a difference in mass would affect the results.
39	B	Number Behavior	According to Table 1, the maximum height reached by both athletes was identical to the initial position of Point X.
40	J	Step Two	Graduate Student 3 states that "gravitational attraction...had no effect on the results."

8.6   Practice Test 1

#	Answer	Skill	Explanation
1	B	Locators	The lines in Figure 1 intersect at a x-axis value of 2005.
2	H	Math	$10 + 20 + 5 + 30 = 65$
3	D	Locators	The passage states that the Asian black bear is one of the main predators of tigers. This implies that, if all Asian black bears are removed, the population of tigers in the region would increase. Figure 1 shows a population of approximately 200 million for tigers in the year 2010. Four years later, if their predator is removed, the tiger population would be higher than 200 million.
4	F	Math	The percent of species in Table 1 add up to 90%. This means the scientists failed to place 10% of tiger species in a Red List category.
5	C	Yes, Yes, No, No	Answer choices B and D, according to Figure 1, have incorrect explanations. The correct explanation agrees with the inverse relationship stated in the question.
6	G	Math	According to Table 1, a total of 25% of tiger species are either Vulnerable (VU) or Endangered (EN). If 300 species were sorted, 25% of 300 equals 75.
7	B	Number Behavior	Figure 2 shows an inverse trend between pressure and λ.
8	F	Locators	At 285 K in Figure 1, Li has a y-axis value of approximately 425 nm, Na a value of 275 nm, K a value of 190 nm, and Rb a value of 160 nm.
9	B	Locators	Sodium (Na) is approximately 125 nm less at any given x-value. For example, at 900 mm Hg, the y-value for Na is approximately 210 nm and the y-value for Li is approximately 330 nm.
10	G	Data Bridge	The order of increasing atomic radii is: Li, Na, K, then Rb. Using this same order, the mean free path decreases according to Figure 1.
11	A	Data Bridge	Cesium would be located below Rb in Table 1. Jumping to Figure 1, at 270 K, the mean free path for Cesium would be lower than that of Rb, which is 150 nm. Answer choice A is the only option lower than 150 nm.

#	Answer	Skill	Explanation
12	J	Yes, Yes, No, No	Answer choices G and H have incorrect explanations. Since Rubidium has the shorter mean free path, the frequency of collisions would be higher.
13	A	Step One	First sentences indicate Scientist 3 is arguing DNA damage accumulation, while Scientist 4 is arguing random DNA mutation. This eliminates answer choices B and D. Scientist 4 mentions that DNA damage causes DNA mutation, not the other way around.
14	F	Yes, Yes, No, No	Answer choices G and H do not match their respective viewpoints. The key phrase of the question is "programmed", which is mentioned by Scientist 2.
15	D	The Irrelevant Argument	Apoptosis is mentioned by Scientist 2, not Scientist 4.
16	H	Step One	Scientist 2 argues life expectancy is predetermined. Random environmental factors, as stated by answer choice H, would contradict that viewpoint.
17	A	Step Two	The last sentences of each viewpoint all state that, at a certain point, life is no longer sustainable.
18	F	Step Two	The key phrase of the question is "antioxidants." The only Scientist that mentions anything resembling antioxidants is Scientist 3, who mentions "oxygen ions" and "peroxides."
19	B	Outside Knowledge	H_2O_2 is hydrogen peroxide. Scientist 3 mentions peroxides cause DNA damage.
20	F	Locators	Figure 1 shows that, at a x-axis value of 120, the y-axis value for one of the data points is approximately 130. This value is 10 units greater.
21	A	Yes, Yes, No, No	Figure 1 shows the results of the NP fertilizer, which are generally higher than the normal fertilizer line. This eliminates answer choices C and D. Answer choice A has the correct explanation.
22	F	Water and Drying	Study 1 mentions the soil was left to dry in the sun. Any mention of drying implies the removal of water or moisture.
23	C	Scientific Method	The type of fertilizer used was intentionally varied between the studies. This eliminates answer chocies A, B, and D.
24	H	Locators	The passage mentions that "active" means the fertilizer increased the lima bean count above normal levels. Figures 1 and 3, which represent fertilizers NP and NPK respectively, display data points above the normal line.
25	C	Yes, Yes, No, No	Answer choices A, B, and D have incorrect explanations. Figure 3, which is the fertilizer containing all three elements, yields the highest quantity of viable lima beans.
26	G	Outside Knowledge	Nitrogen and phosphorous are nonmetals while potassium is a metal. Study 1 did not contain potassium and yielded more viable lima beans than Study 2, which did contain potassium.

#	Answer	Skill	Explanation
27	A	Locators	The last sentence of the passage states charged leptons are electron-like. All 5 leptons in Table 2 have a negative charge.
28	J	Data Bridge	Table 1 shows the proton is composed of two dag-crews and one soh-crew. Adding the masses of these crews: $2.5 + 2.5 + 5.0 = 10.0$ MeV. This does not equal the mass of a proton listed in Table 1.
29	A	Outside Knowledge	The neutron is neutral with a charge of 0. Table 1 shows the neutron is composed of two soh-crews and one dag-crew. Adding the charges of these crews: $-1/3 + -1/3 + 2/3 = 0$.
30	J	Data Bridge	Table 1 shows the Delta-minus trio is composed of three soh-crews. Based on Table 3, this equals a charge of -1. The Omega trio also has a charge of -1.
31	B	Data Bridge	Table 1 indicates the top Lambda trio is composed of one dag-crew, one soh-crew, and one cas-crew. When the cas-crew decays to a brg-crew, the math using Table 3 is as follows: $2/3 + -1/3 + -1/3 = 0$.
32	F	Math	Calculating the total charge for answer choices A, B, C, and D will yield +1, -1, 0, and 0 respectively. A charge of +1 is desired to neutralize the -1 charge of a pan-lepton.
33	D	Math	Each proton has a mass of 1,000 MeV, each neutron has a mass of 1,000 MeV, and each electron has a mass of 0.5 MeV. Hence, $2(1,000) + 2(1,000) + 2(0.5) = 4,001$ MeV.
34	F	Number Behavior	Table 1 shows a direct trend between solution and final mass.
35	C	Locators	A solution of 0.7 g/L in Table 1 would be located between 0.6 g/L and 0.8 g/L, which yielded a difference in mass of 27 and 29 grams respectively.
36	G	Locators	The passages states that 0.02 g of NaCl was mixed with 100 mL of pure H_2O to create a 0.2 g/L solution. A 0.5 g/L solution would use the same amount of water and a similar 0.05 g of NaCl.
37	D	Scientific Method	Table 2 yields much greater differences in mass than Table 1, except for Solution P.
38	H	Yes, Yes, No, No	Answer choices G and J have incorrect explanations. The correct explanation disagrees with the hypothesis of the student.
39	A	Scientific Method	"Intentionally varied" implies the independent variable of the experiment. Since the solution concentration is listed first in Table 1, we can conclude it was purposely changed. The molecule of salt and material of each bag are not stated in the data, which means they were held constant. The difference in mass is measured and the dependent variable.
40	H	Locators	The passage states that osmosis is the net movement of water. This eliminates answer choices A and B. Since water "flows from an area of low solute to an area of high solute", the water would move from the intracellular fluid to the extracellular fluid.

8.7   Practice Test 2

#	ANSWER	SKILL	EXPLANATION
1	A	Locators	Individuals 3 and 5 are siblings, both with normal vision.
2	G	Locators	The key of the pedigree chart lists Individual 6 as a female carrier. The passage states Individual 4, who is also a female carrier, has genotype XX^-.
3	A	Outside Knowledge	A Punnett square is required (XX crossed with X^-Y). All the male children will have normal vision.
4	J	Yes, Yes, No, No	Answer choices F and H have incorrect explanations. A carrier of a recessive trait does not show the dominant phenotype.
5	C	Outside Knowledge	Answer choices B and D have incorrect explanations. Fathers give the Y chromosome to male children. According to the passage, color blindness is located on the X chromosome. This implies all male biological children obtain the disorder from their mothers. Individual 25 has a color blind mother, which would yield a genotype of X^-Y.
6	G	Outside Knowledge	A Punnett square is required (XX^- crossed with XY). Two of the four children have normal vision, one child is a carrier, and the last is color blind.
7	C	Data Bridge	In Table 1, as the soil percentage decreases, the composite number increases. In Figure 2, as the composite number increases, the average plant yield increases then decreases.
8	G	Math	Figure 2 yields an average plant yield for Composite 5 of 3,000 g/plant. Since there are 1,000 grams in 1 kilogram, this would be equal to 3 kg/plant.
9	D	Yes, Yes, No, No	Answer choices A and C have incorrect explanations. The correct explanation disagrees with the student's hypothesis.
10	F	Scientific Method	Table 1 shows that 0% of broiler litter was used in Composite 1. This is the standard of comparison for all composites in the studies.
11	C	Locators	Study 1 states that 100 days elapsed, while Study 2 states that 150 days elapsed. The introduction specifies the scientific name of both the avocado and eggplant.
12	J	Scientific Method	Answer choices F and G can be eliminated since Studies 1 and 2 are measuring the *average* plant yield. The quantity of seeds is irrelevant.
13	D	Outside Knowledge	Fruits primarily contain sugars. $C_6H_{12}O_6$ is the chemical formula for glucose.
14	F	Number Behavior	Figure 3 shows a direct trend between time and oxygen concentration.
15	D	Math	Figure 1 shows the oxygen concentration reached 2 mg/m^3 10 hours after the experiment started. Based on the description of Study 1, the experiment began at 6:00 A.M. 10 hours after 6:00 A.M. is 4:00 P.M.
16	J	Yes, Yes, No, No	Answer choices F and H have incorrect explanations. The correct explanation disagrees with the statement in the question. Figure 2 has the highest oxygen concentration at 24 hours.

#	Answer	Skill	Explanation
17	D	Cannot Be Determined	Study 1 mentions 2-5 grams of leaves were used, but not the exact quantity of leaves.
18	G	Scientific Method	The glass box ensures the plants will be exposed to sunlight.
19	B	Locators	Figure 1 shows the oxygen concentration inside of the box containing snake plant leaves increases rapidly 10-15 hours after the start of the experiment. Since the experiment began at 6:00 A.M., 10-15 hours after that time would be 4:00 P.M. - 9:00 P.M.
20	F	Yes, Yes, No, No	Answer choices G and J have incorrect explanations. The correct explanation agrees with the introductory information.
21	B	Outside Knowledge	Experiment 2 states the procedure from Experiment 1 was repeated. In Experiment 1, the students began with pure water, which has a pH of 7.
22	H	Locators	Experiment 3 states "4 Solutions (A-D) of unknown pH" were tested. Experiments 1 and 2 test known pH samples.
23	B	Locators	The passage states that the transition range is "where a color change occurs". According to Table 1, methyl orange is changing color between a pH of 3-5.
24	J	Yes, Yes, No, No	Answer choices F and H have incorrect explanations. The correct explanation states that phenolphthalein is 2 different colors at the desired pH values, which is desirable for differentiating between 2 solutions.
25	C	Locators	All answer choice explanations are correct. According to Table 3, Solution A has a "Y-Y-X-G" pattern with respect to the 4 pH indicators. This pattern is also shown in Table 1 for a pH of 5. Hence, Solution A has a pH close to 5. This eliminates answer choices A and B. Answer choice D would not help to differentiate between a pH of 3-4, as stated in the question, and a pH of 5.
26	G	Locators	Solution B in Table 3 has a "Y-B-P-G" pattern. This same pattern also appears for pH values 9-13 in Table 2. Using this logic, Solution A would have a pH of 5, Solution C a pH of 4, and Solution D a pH of 7. Solution B has the most uncertainty in determining its pH.
27	C	Inverse Trends	The highest pOH would equate to the lowest pH. Since Solution C has the lowest pH (see solution for Question 26) it would have the highest pOH.
28	G	Step One	The first sentence of Student 1 states an inverse relationship between speed and mass.
29	D	Step One	Answer choices B and C have incorrect explanations. The correct explanation for Student 2 would agree that the heavier object, the bowling ball, would reach the surface first.
30	H	Step One	The first sentences of both Students 1 and 2 state that mass affects the movement of the objects. Student 3 states that mass "becomes obsolete" when manipulating the force equations.
31	A	Math	The force due to gravity of Object A would be: $F_g = 10 \text{ kg} \times 9.8 \text{ m/s}^2 = 98 \text{ N}.$

#	Answer	Skill	Explanation
32	G	Step Two	Student 3 states,"if any physical factors, such as friction, are unequally distributed" on the inclined plane, that it would result in a difference in fall time. The question states that the friction is equally distributed. This would not change the viewpoint of Student 3, which argues both objects will reach the bottom at the exact same time.
33	A	Step One	Student 1 argues lighter objects move faster. Since Object D is heavier than Object C, Object C will move faster according to Student 1 and reach the bottom of the inclined plane first.
34	J	Step Two	Student 3 states "the mass of each object becomes obsolete when correctly deducing the force equations." Since the only other variable in Newton's second law is acceleration, we can conclude that the acceleration of both objects must be equal to result in equal fall times.
35	J	Number Behavior	Table 2 shows that as the value for L increases by 10 m, the value for x increases by 2.5 cm. Hence, a L of 50 m results in a x of 12.5 cm, and furthermore, a L of 60 m resulting in a x of 15.0 cm.
36	F	Scientific Method	The students are recording bands of light which appear on a piece of paper. The darker the room in which the experiment is being conducted, the easier to see the band patterns.
37	D	Scientific Method	The independent variable typically appears first in tables and is intentionally varied in equal intervals. The dependent variable typically appears to the right in tables and is measured.
38	F	Anticipating the Extra Step	Experiment 2 shows a direct trend between L and x. In Experiment 3 L equals 10 m. If L were instead 5 m, this would result in a decrease of all values of x based on the trend identified in Table 2. This leaves answer choice A as the correct answer.
39	C	Outside Knowledge	Table 1 shows an inverse trend between d and x, Table 2 shows a direct trend between L and x, and Table 3 shows a direct trend between λ and x. In a variation equation, variables with a direct relationship with x are placed in the numerator, while variables with an inverse relationships with x are placed in the denominator.
40	J	Math	The distance from the slits to the band pattern is $L = 10$ m, or 1,000 cm. The distance between the n = 0 and n = 4 band, in Trial 3, is 0.83 cm. The angle generated from the double slit paper, from n = 0 to n = 4, would be inside of a right triangle with opposite side 0.83 cm and adjacent side 10 m. The trig function that uses the opposite and adjacent sides is tangent. This eliminates answer choices F and G. In addition, answer choices F and H could be eliminated because they fail to convert L into centimeters. This leaves answer choice J.

CHAPTER 9

STUDENT PAGES

Homework Assignments

NOTES

ABOUT THE AUTHOR

Michael Cerro graduated from The Cooper Union for the Advancement of Science and Art with a Bachelor's and Master's in Chemical Engineering. He has been passionate about teaching since high school, where he tutored math and science regents preparation for families who could not afford private instruction.

He has conducted over 4,000 private lessons helping students improve their standardized test scores on the ACT, SAT, and SAT II subject tests in math, biology, and chemistry. Michael is the Resource Development Director and oversees all content creation and revisions for Private Prep. In addition, as part of the curriculum team, Michael helps train incoming tutors on the latest strategies in ACT math and science.

Michael resides in Long Island, New York. He is a lover of all sports, a P90X graduate, and lifelong chess player.

ABOUT PRIVATE PREP

Private Prep is a premier educational services company offering individually customized lessons for a wide range of Pre-K through college-level subjects, executive functioning, standardized test prep, and college admissions consulting. Each family works with a personal Education Director, who is always available to provide support and resources in navigating the academic journey. Our Academic Coaches work one-on-one with students designing curriculum for each student's unique learning style. Coaches are experienced, passionate, and highly qualified educators with a track record of success helping students improve grades and increase test scores, as well as build confidence and develop valuable study skills that last a lifetime.

As a company, we seek to embody our core values on every level. Our commitment to personal and professional development, a culture of caring, entrepreneurship, and innovation enables us to provide a unique and vibrant place in the education industry. In 2014, Private Prep was recognized by Crain's NY as one of the '100 Best Places to Work' and has been ranked in the top 15 on Inc. 5000's national list of 'Fastest Growing Private Companies' in Education for the past three years – 2013, 2014, and 2015.

Our operations span the Tri-State area, Washington DC, and Los Angeles. We deliver a high touch education experience that is supported by diverse and excellent resources in recruitment, curriculum design, professional training, and custom software development.

Made in the USA
Lexington, KY
21 June 2016